TESTIMONIALS — MAXIMIZE YOUR SUCCESS

When Jordan asked me to have a look at his new compilation book, I said yes. (I always say yes to Jordan; he's a great friend and one of the most giving people I know.) I'm so glad he asked me! In just a few short chapters, it became clear that this was a book that needed writing. Each chapter is an essay by a successful network marketer, and each is a heartfelt, honest, and wise telling of that person's story, their values, and their beliefs. What we get from the sharing these generous souls were kind enough to provide is the powerful truth, that highly successful people are just like you and me. They're real people with real concerns, real challenges, and real inner demons. But what distinguishes each of them is a set of principles and practices that have allowed them to rise above their challenges and to find the opportunity for growth. When you hear about their journey, you'll be inspired to learn how ordinary people can do extraordinary things by managing their habits and attitudes. Read it and you'll be changed!

Dr. Steve Taubman
Bestselling Author of *UnHypnosis for Network Marketers* and *Bulletproof*

Momentum Makers is a book of extraordinary stories written by ordinary people that had dreams and were willing to work for them. Whether you're just starting out as an entrepreneur or not, it's likely you'll see yourself in some of these stories. This book has compiled amazing stories that illustrate the heart of entrepreneurship.

Dr. Ivan Misner
Founder of BNI and NYT Best-Selling Author

One of the BEST ways we remember and learn is through stories, and *Momentum Makers* has done an amazing job putting together stories of "real average people" that are making it in network marketing.

These "average people" didn't have any special advantage but each one of them "made it" in their own unique way.

This book gives you countless ideas, lessons and inspiration on how to grow your network marketing business. It'll also build your belief to a whole new level.

I highly recommend that every person in our profession read this book.

Simon Chan
Consistency Coach / Founder of MLM Nation

This book is an eye-opener with real stories from real people. I loved that the stories didn't feel like cliché fantasy rags-to-riches stories. They aren't about that lucky person who made a fortune, fired her boss, bought the red Ferrari and are living like royalty on a private island. Each story is different and I felt like I learned something special from every one of them. The biggest takeaway for me was that Network Marketing is the greatest equalizer. For every superstar you hear or read about, there are thousands more using this extra income stream to pay for their car, mortgage, college, food and/or family vacations. Network Marketing can truly be a life-changing experience.

Now go write your chapter and hopefully that extra money each month will help make your financial stress disappear. Wouldn't that be nice?

Dave Wilkerson
Host of 2BSRadio.com

I can relate to everyone that contributed to this book. It has captured my attention immediately. The stories are wonderful and uplifting. This book is filled with cheerleaders that will motivate and inspire you.

Everyone was able to create success and proved that it can be achieved when you are under the most challenging times in your life.

This book was so enjoyable and has appropriate timing during our 2020 challenge we are all in.

Their stories are messages or reminders to focus, don't lose your drive and don't lose the belief in yourself.

Jan A. Bruso
Artist - Entrepreneur

If you want more out of life, the personal stories from people like you in this book will tell you you can, and the tips from them will show you the way.

Max Fleischer
Tennis Pro

If you are looking for inspiration and motivation, you will find it in this book. Each story gives you insight into how leaders think and act differently to get bigger and better results. The "key activations" at the end of each chapter make taking action easy and the real-life stories give you the motivation to build the momentum you desire.

Kelley Dominguez
Executive Director, BNI

The way I see it, this book illustrates 2 key points. The first is that Network Marketing is the gateway drug into entrepreneurship. The second is that your success is directly correlated to how quickly you can accelerate your level of personal development. Save yourself years of learning curve and learn from these outstanding stories and testimonials!

Ian Lenhart
Podcasting Expert

As an Executive of National public and private Companies in traditional business models for decades, and now a CEO for a Network Marketing company, I find the stories in this book to be a refreshing and accurate representation of Network Marketing. In that it takes hard consistent work, it has great opportunities for multiple income sources and most of all, it is about your relationships and having a servant leader's heart. Whether your interest is in the gig economy or if you want to replace your entire income stream, I would recommend you read *Momentum Makers* and get real-life stories from these successful entrepreneurs.

Gregg Bryars
Chief Executive Officer SendOutCards

MOMENTUM MAKERS

Over 100 Network Marketing Success Tips From Average People Who Made It BIG!

A Network Marketing Book By Beach Money Publications

Beach Money
PUBLICATIONS

Published by Beach Money Publications
9885 Wyecliff Drive, Suite 200
Highlands Ranch, CO 80126
BeachMoneyPublications.com

Contributing Authors:
Kate Horwitz, Sandi & Ed Cohen, Allen Fu, Mona Christensen, Nina Alexander, Hilari & Justin Courtney, Pille Kapetanakis, Tracy Rodgers, Jordan Adler, Darla Digrandi-Aguilera, Laura Wells, Jaime Peca, Peter & Susie Bagwell, Kelly Bryant, Laurie Delk-Radecki, Christy Fechser, Claudia Stepan, Jo Epere, Victoria McKew, Alicia Pesina, Heather McCloskey, Natasha Roberson, Scott Campbell, Elise Lininger

Manufactured in the United States of America.

ISBN: 978-1-62865-791-3

Contents

FOREWORD

It was 1987, my mother and father had sold their traditional business for pennies on the dollar. They decided to put a deposit down on a five-bedroom house with the view to live in one bedroom and rent the others out to complete strangers.

The rooms filled up very quickly with complete strangers, it was awkward.

Whilst they were living there they got the news that they were pregnant with their first child, me. They were excited, but their situation and living arrangements wasn't so great to bring a new born into.

One day, my father woke up, got out of bed and walked to the bathroom whilst rubbing his cloudy morning eyes. As he opened the door he heard a scream from one of the tenants as they were doing their morning business on the toilet.

Frustrated by the fact he had to wait to use his own bathroom he went downstairs. With every step he took there was an overwhelming feeling of enough is enough. What am I going to do when my child is born? Something has to change.

As he walked into the kitchen he noticed a picture of an Aston Martin sports car in an opened newspaper that was left by one of the tenants lay on the table. The car grabbed his attention but it was three words that had him hooked!

MLM MLM MLM! I drive an Aston Martin, you can too, call me now.

"What could MLM mean?" my father asked himself.

"Ahh I've got it! Make Love Monthly!"

He decided to give the number on the ad a call. Someone on the other end answered and they began a discussion around what my Dad believed was to make love monthly.

After being corrected, this complete stranger carefully explained what the Multi Level Marketing (now known as Network Marketing) business model actually was. My dad, still half asleep, wasn't really following. But he asked for more information. He was invited to an event that was happening an hour away from where he lived and was asked to bring my mother.

On 26th October 1987, my mother, father and I were witnessing our first ever Network Marketing presentation. In fact, I was in the room, in the womb.

Since that day everything changed.

My father had the vehicle to provide the life he wanted for this family. Although he wasn't the smartest man, he knew if others have done it, he could do it too.

Over the years he learned the skills and matched it with a strong work ethic to earn millions of dollars, travel the world with his entire family, help thousands become financially free and become someone of significance.

However, something else happened to him, without realising and it will happen to you too if you take this profession seriously.

As his son, growing up around him building his empire, I witnessed the sacrifice and struggles he went through. At first I thought he was being selfish, putting his business first and not leaving much time left for my brother and me.

I felt he was giving his best to the business, and the rest to me.

Then everything changed.

We were visiting my grandparents in the south of the UK and my dad called us in to the conservatory. It was a rainy day and you could hear each rain drop crash against the glass ceiling.

He said "we are going to play a game".

We were all excited, what could it be?

"We are going to list all the things we would want, as a family, if we were to build our dream home" my dad said excitedly.

Julie, my mum, went first. "I would love a big kitchen". My dad added it to the list.

Frazer, you're next. "I would love a TV in my bedroom". It was added to the list.

Corbyn, my brother, was next. "I would love a snooker table". It was added.

We went around the room filling a piece of paper with everything we wanted. We started to visualise our very own dream home. Then I realised something. My Dad hadn't added anything to the list, it was just mother, my brother and me who shouted out things and he noted them down.

"Dad, why haven't you added anything?"

I remember his answer as if it was yesterday.

"Well, my dream home is the one that you want me to build. I only want you to be happy, that's my dream."

He wasn't being selfish when building his business. He was being selfless. Everything he was doing was for his family!

He then asked us a question which would change the game for our entire family.

"Right, we have a decision to make as a family. I can either use all my spare time with you and we continue living the life we are living or I can use some of that spare time for the next 10 years and we will have the dream home. What shall we do?"

A few seconds went by before we all agreed we wanted the dream home. It was decided, Dad would get busy building the business and we would support him every single step of the way.

As the years went by after that life-changing meeting in the conservatory, we would ask him for updates. Some days were amazing, some weren't so good. Sometimes he was on top of the world, others you knew to just leave him on his own.

8 years after we had decided as a family to get the dream home my Dad shouted for us to all join him in the garage.

We got into the car and we started to drive to an unknown destination, even my mum had no idea where we were headed.

Now, we lived in a village called Formby. There was a road called "Millionaires Row" where all the football players and millions lived. It was one of the most desired roads to live on in the UK at one point.

We started to drive towards the famous road. You could feel the energy in the car fill with excitement. Something was going on, my Dad was smiling from ear to ear. My Mum kept asking where are we going. My brother kept saying are we going to the dream home.

We were getting closer to the most desired place to live in the UK. We were now two roads away. Left turn, now one road away. Right turn.

We were on the famous road!

As we drove passed the houses we were looking at all the mansions that belonged to our favourite football players. Then the car stopped.

My Dad pointed to what looked like a house that hadn't been lived in for years and said "there you go, welcome to the dream home!"

We were confused, it wasn't like all the other houses, surely we couldn't live here.

Then my Dad said "don't worry, we are going to knock that house down, and build the dream home, here is a picture of what it will look like", as he unscrolled an artist's drawing of the plans he had made.

Wow! It looked incredible, it was huge!

Two years went by and it was time for us to move in. We were all so excited.

We pulled up to the house again and as we stood outside in front of the big 10 foot gates my Dad pulled out a piece of paper. It was an off-white colour.

It was the piece of paper that we used 10 years ago to write down all of the things we had listed as a family for our dream home.

I couldn't believe it, had he actually done it?

My Dad looked so proud, my Mum was overwhelmed with emotion and I was simply shocked.

"Right, before we go explore the new house, I want us to go around together and tick off all the things we have on this list one by one" my Dad said calmly.

We walked up the drive.

The 3 door garage. Tick. The big bonsai tree. Tick. The big glass windows. Tick. The glass front door. Tick.

We went inside. The marble floors. Tick. The double sided staircase. Tick. The snooker table. Tick. TV in every bedroom. Tick. Huge kitchen. Tick.

This went on until everything on the list we had written was ticked.

That was the moment that my Mum and Dad became my heroes.

I believe true success is when the people you mentor in this world tell you honestly that you are their hero.

Network Marketing gives you the chance to create a life you can dream of. You are going to be reading a number of stories from some of the best people in the industry today. Not only have their lives changed through the income they have created, but the impact they are having on the world is helping make it a better place.

Jordan Adler is someone who many call their hero. His message has been told all over the world through his books and powerful presentations. He is someone I look up to, seek advice from, and am beyond grateful to call a friend.

KATE HORWITZ

NO ONE GETS OUT ALIVE

That title was meant to stop you in your tracks. What in the heck am I talking about? I'm talking about life, this life and your life. Complacency is our biggest threat. Why? Because we don't live forever. Yet, we live our lives as if we have all the time in the world. While it's true, some of us have many decades on this earth; other people's time is significantly shorter. The truth is no one has any idea how much time they have, or how much time their loved ones have. That thought brings me to one of my favorite quotes by Leo Christopher, "There's only one thing more precious than our time and that's who we spend it on." My passion is helping people realize that their time is limited and providing them with a solution that gives them more options in their life and more choices on how they choose to spend their time.

How I discovered my passion might surprise you. I'm married to an amazing man, John. We have 3 grown kids. Having worked as a CPA with very long hours and great commitments, I felt very lucky to choose to be a stay-at-home mom when my oldest went to kindergarten. I loved my "mom life" and threw myself into my kids' lives. I was the treasurer of the PTA/PTO for many years. I filled my days with tennis matches, kids' activities and I even went part time to Culinary School at the community college. My life was busy. Life was AMAZING until one day in 2010 when I looked in the mirror and wondered who the person was looking back at me and how did she get so old?

I grew up in Hawaii and all those years of sailing the Pacific had finally showed up on my face as sun damage and wrinkles. Coincidently, at the same time, a friend had invited me to her skincare business launch event, and I was formally introduced to Network Marketing. I was intrigued and thought maybe this was what I was looking for, but I didn't have much knowledge of the brand. So, I asked a friend what she knew about it. I was surprised to learn that she used the products and she raved about her results. Based on what she said, I decided I wanted to try it.

So, I attended my friend's event and after looking over the products, I decided I wanted three of the four regimens, two for me and one for my daughter. When I was told the price for the product, I figured there was a big discount to join (there was) and I have a black belt in shopping, so it was a no brainer. More stuff, less money, sign me up! I never even asked my husband, nor did I consult with anyone. I simply joined for the discount; I had no intention of running a business, ever, and I told my friend that. I didn't think I needed the money… Famous last words. I just wanted to be a wholesale buyer.

When I got home, I confessed to my husband that I had become a consultant. He encouraged me in only a way a husband can, "None of our friends will ever talk to us again." Hahahaha. I told him he didn't know what he was talking about and besides, I had no intention of actually selling products. But after I joined, two things happened that altered my direction with this company. The first big change was that the products really worked! I could actually feel my skin changing. The second thing was that I noticed my friend was having FUN. Say what? She was having fun doing this business. Now that got my attention. I wanted to have fun. Somewhere along the way, my life had lost its fun factor. So I called her up and asked, "what am I missing"? I attended an event with her, which was fun. I met so many new friends and I learned what I needed to do to build a business. Use the products, share your results, and reach out consistently to people to see if they are open to taking a look at the opportunity or the products. That sounded like something I could do, share something I loved with others. After hearing that, I was all in! Sign me up. Well, I was already signed up.

My decision that day to build a business altered the course of my life. In my first six days in business, I made back the cost of my starter kit. In fact, I've been profitable ever since. In addition to missing the fun quotient, just as I started my business, my son decided he wanted to chase his dream of playing ice hockey. In his case, that meant leaving home at sixteen and attending boarding school in Minnesota. We had never planned for or even considered boarding school for our kids, so his dream was an expensive reality and that extra cash I was making came in handy.

The years passed and the other kids had dreams of their own (our daughter went to a semester of high school in Israel and our youngest son went to boarding school in Florida) and the extra money grew. It wasn't life-changing income, but it was a steady stream of income that I counted on. One thing that's certain is I could never have been present for my kids in three different states, or chased them around the world if I had created a secondary stream of income from a traditional job. In my opinion, network marketing presents a better quality of life than any other alternative career because of its flexibility. For many years, I thought my 'why' for building my business, was to bring in a secondary stream of income to offset the cost of three kids chasing their dreams. But about a year ago, a good friend, Tracy, pointed out my true 'why.' (Sometimes others can see things that you don't.) Once it was pointed out to me, I knew I had found my truth – I exist to motivate others to maximize the time they have in order to accomplish their dreams. My friend helped me see that this purpose was rooted in the DNA of who I am because of where I had been so many years before. Like so many others, the pain of what happened in my life had quietly become my success driver.

I came from a large, merged family with six kids. I was one of the two youngest and there was a 20-year gap between my brother and I, and our older siblings. While most of us lived near each other, we never lived together. In fact, I'm closer in age to their kids than I am to them. By the time I was 40, I had lost my immediate family. My dad died from cancer at 72 when I was just 20 years old. Rich, the brother closest to me in age, died from cancer at 34 and my Mom died from a stroke at 83 when I was 40. My Mom's death was sudden and for the first time in my life, this type A personality had trouble coping. I thought I knew what to expect since I had already experienced the death of my Dad and Rich, but I was so very wrong.

When my mom died, my immediate thought was last man standing. Everyone who I had lived with growing up was gone. I was bereft and felt like an abandoned house with broken windows and torn curtains blowing in the wind. It took me a long time to learn to live with her death. But her death, maybe because I was now alone, taught me that life is short. I thought, "Does this matter?" My husband and I made different choices after her death. He left an unsatisfying career. We moved back to Hawaii and into my childhood home. We spent time together, as a family. Choices we would have never made if I hadn't lost my mom. When I joined my company, my mom had been gone for six years. Personally, I had been focused on living my best life for those six years. But until Tracy brought it to my attention, I didn't understand my true why.

I fell into network marketing and enjoyed helping people restore their confidence by solving their skin concerns. That was certainly gratifying, but now, my passion is helping people realize that time is their most precious asset and I have a solution, through my business, to give them more opportunity in their lives.

While network marketing is hard work, I believe it is the only option that has a low cost of entry, unlimited income potential, and can be worked around a full-time career and busy life. Lots of people have dreams or want more out of their lives, they just don't know how to get from where they are to where they want to be. People feel stuck. Their dreams might be so big that they seem impossible. But nobody climbs a mountain in one step. The mountain is conquered one step at a time. It's all about the journey.

My job is to show what's possible through network marketing and to make it simple for my team. Notice, I didn't say easy, I said simple; there's a difference. If it were easy, everybody would do it. A lot of my job concerns mindset, my own and the mindset of my team and potential business partners. People might have a lot of objections with this industry. People have a lot of fear about network marketing, it's not the normal career path and it isn't what we were taught growing up. It's my job to talk with people and discover WHY they think the way they do and to show them that this business might be just what they need. This business isn't for everyone, but it is a brilliant business model that provides the opportunity for income, personal growth, community and FUN!

What started as a way for me to get the biggest discount on the skincare products I wanted, gave me the vision for something bigger. So what has this decision done? It's helped 100s of people over nine and a half years love their skin and regain their confidence. This business has given me amazing skin, incredible experiences, cool gifts and the ability to impact more lives working from anywhere I may be in the world. It's given me myself back. So that is how I ended up here. This is my unique story. It's a story of what's possible with consistency, hard work and vision. The question is, how can I be of service to you?

Have a vision for your life and focus on where you are going, not where you are. Make small changes in your mindset and in your routine. Start where you are and take imperfect action. Evaluate your progress and make course corrections along the way. Your life is about the journey. There is no destination. If you're afraid or nervous, you just might be on the right track. Change happens when you're uncomfortable. So just begin. Start TODAY. Stop waiting for the right time. There is no right time, there is just today.

MOMENTUM MAKERS

1. **NEVER LET LIFE LOSE ITS FUN FACTOR:** Life should not be redundant, feel like a struggle and boring. If you feel this way, you need to change things. Find something you LOVE! There will always be a business opportunity in the things you love. Don't allow yourself to settle for less just because it's in front of you. Find the thing that is worth your life investment.

2. **FIND YOUR WHY:** Deep in you there is a specific passion that drives why you pursue the things you pursue. It could be that the world sucks and you want to change it. Or, it could be that the way something is done seems broken and unproductive and you want to make it better. Whatever it is, find the thing that makes you tick and drives your ambitions. When you connect with whatever that is, it will make you successful.

3. **BE A DREAM MAKER:** Everyone loves helping others. Sometimes our life can get so focused on the things we want that we lose sight of helping those around us accomplish their wants. Find a way to help others accomplish their dreams. Doing so will help you discover your own passions.

SANDI AND ED COHEN

LIVE A LIBERATED LIFE

Are you looking for more time freedom?

Are you looking for financial Peace of Mind?

Do you want to wake up every morning with a feeling of Joy and Gratitude and loving where you are versus where you have to be?

All of this is possible, not because I'm saying it is but because I've lived it. We have lived life both ways. We pursued the normal, expected road to success, getting an education, working in industry, growing traditional businesses and we have also lived life in a non-traditional occupation – the profession of Network Marketing. Both worked; but only the latter has produced true freedom.

Ed and I grew up as childhood sweethearts. We went to the same college and eventually became business partners and yes, we are still together. We're the best of friends and love doing all of life together.

It seems like yesterday when we met when I was 15 years old, braces on my teeth, and Ed starting Temple University Pharmacy school. Often we tell people, "Life is like a roll of toilet paper. The closer you get to the end, the faster it goes." While our life seems to be moving at record speed, we are where we want to be.

How fast is time flying for you? Are you now where you thought you could be?

If we were to have a conversation with our teenaged selves, our journey to the profession of Network Marketing would be an incredible and unexpected surprise. No one wakes up one day and says, "I want to be a network marketer." Often, there is a compelling reason for wanting change.

Our story is different than most success stories. We went from Riches to Rags and back to Riches by helping others.

When I graduated from Temple University with a BS in Education, I volunteered to be the first white female teacher in Philadelphia, PA at an elementary school during the days of integration. Martin Luther King was one of my heroes. I wanted to make a difference! It was my intention to have a positive impact on others wherever and whenever I could.

Eventually, Ed had 5 pharmacies and in 1978, one customer could not get needed supplies for her mother from another pharmacy; so, I started a Medical and Surgical supply business in the front part of one of his stores. Within 3 years, I had a multimillion-dollar business servicing Pennsylvania, New Jersey, and Delaware with my specialty, pediatrics: children with special needs.

We worked hard, 24 hours a day 7 days a week, with 6 trucks on the street, a million dollars in receivables and half a million dollars in inventory. Success was achieved! As a result of the commitment to be of service to others, we were able to buy our 10,000 square foot dream home, which was beautifully furnished. In the driveway was a Corvette, a Rolls Royce and a stretch limo. We had an English houseman as well as a cook from Grand Cayman. We never thought our dream life would ever go away.

In Dr. M. Scott Peck's book, *THE ROAD LESS TRAVELED*, the first 3 words are LIFE IS DIFFICULT.

We had no idea what that really meant until, in 1986, we sold our business to a group of accountants and attorneys who were looking for an investment. About 7 months after the acquisition, the new owners defaulted and breached our legal agreements and a nightmare in the Philadelphia court system began.

It took us 8 years to finally get our day in court. We never missed an episode of LA LAW and even watched reruns. We spent 2 days selecting a jury. As the trial was ready to begin, the judge became extremely angry at the people who had PURCHASED our company and stated, "THE COHENS HAVE BEEN HARMED ENOUGH. I AM NOT GOING TO PERMIT A LENGTHLY, EXPENSIVE, COMPLICATED TRIAL THAT WILL BE TOO HARD FOR THE JURORS TO UNDERSTAND," and he pierced the corporate veil and forced a settlement. While a settlement avoided the high costs of a trial, it was terribly small because the business was now bankrupt. The only winners were the attorneys.

We were dead right, dead broke and $450K in debt. We had to start our lives all over again from ground zero. If you were 52 years old and $450K in debt and lost everything you worked so hard to build, what would you do?

We decided to move west to Arizona, to see sunshine and start our lives over. When you are in a downward spiral, you think it will never end, and it usually gets worse before it gets better. My mother, who was living in Florida, had breast cancer and the beginnings of Alzheimer's and we brought her to live with us and I became her full-time caregiver. She was being tube fed, on oxygen, and diapered several times a day. Our financial struggle was so bad that the only reason they did not shut off our electric service was because Mom was on life support.

We had gone from driving a Rolls Royce to sharing a 9-year-old car with no air conditioning …in Arizona, in the summer. Shortly after arriving in Arizona, I was introduced to a friend I still have today who eventually became my business partner. She had achieved great success in real estate, and told me, "if you are willing to help others, you might get your life back" through leveraged income.

Similar to Ed and me, she had found great success in building a traditional real estate business; however, she found herself wanting more time freedom. I had promised Ed that I would never do Network Marketing again after I had convinced him to purchase $8,000 of water filters that we tried to sell in our pharmacies unsuccessfully. However, I did not have options and I needed to find a way to create income working from home. It was then that I started my new journey in the profession of Network Marketing.

When I began in Network Marketing over 27 years ago, I was so frustrated, and my husband was so negative in the belief that it was possible to succeed. I saw people having success and kept thinking, "what do they say and do to create duplication?" I became a serious student, believing my success was possible.

What a huge learning curve!

Those first couple of years in Network Marketing were frustrating, trying to understand how to choose a company, owners, product/service, and compensation plan. We went through 11 companies in about 2 ½ years before "cracking the code" and finding the right fit for us. The experience was hard and tiresome; but the experience we got during those first few years cannot be replaced. It is what would eventually propel us into our success. It is now 2019, and we have only been involved in 2 companies in 24 years. The most important thing we've accomplished in those 24 years has been the impact and influence we bring to others.

Over the years, we have worked with thousands of people who believe they want a better life; however, there is a difference between dreaming about it and pursuing it. Getting to your life goals requires great sacrifice and a willingness to make real change. So many people want a better way of life but are not willing to spend at least 7-10 hours a week to improve their skills and make their dreams a reality.

People often ask, what's the secret to success in Network Marketing? The answer is always the same. Success comes from developing your skills, which will be in direct proportion to your income.

It's very important to understand that every business requires work. In the work, some will fail, and some will succeed. Every industry has failures. Network Marketing is no exception. The people who figure out how to push through difficulties to stay focused on their production are the ones who make it.

Life is about choices. You will either choose to live a disappointed life filled with all of the things that keep you from attaining what you want; or, you will choose to set aside temporary distractions to get the life you want to live.

Over the course of our nearly 30 years in business as network marketers, we have learned some valuable lessons.

Master the Art of Asking Questions. To determine how we can help people get to a place of joy and gratitude we must ask questions. We are NOT salespeople. We are PROBLEM SOLVERS! To find success, you must be more interested in how you impact someone else's life than how they impact yours. You cannot really know how to positively contribute to someone else if you do not take the time to really understand him or her. Ask more questions than you answer.

Practice the Law of Intention. For example, before I pick up the phone to make a call, a 3-way call, Zoom, or meet with someone, I anticipate a positive outcome. Before you go to bed at night, know your schedule of activities for the next day. Commit to 90-day massive action sprints and work like your life depends on it. In short – Always Be Planning. Success without intention is just an accident. It cannot be repeated and will likely be squandered. Planned success creates building blocks for a desired life.

Language Matters. Most people rarely explore below the surface of their own lives. Key phrases can help you help others unlock dreams they did not even realize they had. Some examples include:

- Would it be OK to?
- Would anything stop you from getting started right away IF you love what you see?
- Can you imagine?
- What impressed you the most about what you looked at?
- If I send you information now, when can you commit to reviewing and let's set up a follow up now to be sure we get any questions answered. Fair enough?

Focusing questions on open-ended opportunities for others helps them break through the stuckness they feel in their life to be free to explore what could be.

Invitation Outweighs Persuasion. People do not want to be "sold". They love to join things they see as successful. They want to jump into something that is attractive. When building your business, you should INVITE and NOT SELL to determine if they are "OPEN" to wanting or needing what you offer. Practically, that means inviting someone to "hear what you're doing." Asking them for their thoughts and opinions will stir questions in their mind that they will want answers to. Telling someone how great something is robs him or her of discovery. Remember – you are here to serve them.

We are now in a new chapter of our lifelong passion to make a difference. This now includes helping others live the life of their dreams by using the Mastermind principle AND USING THE HIGHEST OF TECHNOLOGY TOOLS TO ACCELERATE GROWTH. If you are curious about our new chapter OF ENDEVOUR, just reach out to us.

All successful people have a story…just maybe we can help you create yours. Reach out if you would like a complimentary 30-minute session.

We just love making new friends.

You are where your thoughts are.

Make sure your thoughts are where you want to be.

> "Talent alone won't make you a success.
> Neither will being in the right place at the right time, unless you are ready.
> The most important question is,
> ARE YOU READY?"
> - Johnny Carson

MOMENTUM MAKERS

1. **TIME MATTERS:** Time is the most valuable asset we have. We cannot get more of it. As such, we do not have time to waste. We must be intentional with every moment we have. There is a difference between enjoying deserved downtime and wasting time.

2. **PEOPLE MATTER:** Everyone in your life matters. They have worth and value even if they cannot help you grow your business. In today's fast-paced, high demand world, it can be easy for us to lose intentionality in our relationships. Take the time to focus on the people around you. Don't build your business on the backs of broken relationships.

3. **YOU MATTER:** You must be intentional in developing yourself. You are the captain of your ship. If you are not intentional with how you develop yourself, you will never be fully satisfied with your life.

ALLEN FU

FAMILY, FUN & FORTUNE

Leveraging the Immigrant Mentality to Network Marketing Success – Allen Fu

My story as a network marketer transcends my own personal story, it is one of family, hardship and overcoming adversity. I hope that it inspires you.

My parents met as non-English speaking immigrants in Australia. Having emigrated from China, they had chased the same dream that so many others had before them – a better life, including their own home, education for kids they would someday have and the freedom that democratic society brings. When they eventually met, however, their lives looked very different than their expectations. They were both working as many as 3 back-to-back jobs, labouring 16-18 hours per day and hardly making enough money to put food on the table.

After falling in love and getting married, they both had dreams of entrepreneurialism – but, how would that ever be possible for 2 people living in a country that did not speak their language, fearful every day of losing their job or of being swindled. They worked hard. They pressed on. They saved.

Eventually, they were able to launch a small retail business working at weekend markets. That business eventually grew to multiple brick and mortar locations across Sydney, Australia. But, like every small business owner, the need for cash flow in the business keeps the owner trapped in a sea of inconsistency. Eventually, my parents were exhausted and desperate for the freedom they had so much desired. Thankfully they possessed the immigrant mentality – an attitude for life and work that wired them to seek out and take all sorts of opportunities. With crisis around every corner, they were tuned to deal with adversity, be resourceful and do whatever it takes to overcome it. It was this mentality that allowed me to be who I am today.

In 2003, mum was introduced to Network Marketing. I suffered from sinusitis, an exacerbated inflammation of the sinuses. Imagine, being allergic to the planet to the point of having no sense of smell for 8 years! A mother at our local acupuncture clinic was coincidentally a customer of ours at one of our shoe stores and she recognised me doing homework in the shop one day. Strangely enough, her son had the same issue as me and she had just started using products from this company and they seemed to help. She recommended the products to my mum and without a second of hesitation my mum enrolled. My father was very skeptical. He had heard all about Network Marketing's history of illegitimacy. He did not trust that a business with no physical presence could be a real business. He shunned my mom's efforts and continued the path of working hard to develop what he understood, although living a very unsatisfied life.

To this day, I am impressed that my mum was able to build a business behind my dad's back whilst being aware of his disapproval of the profession. She made a promise to herself to not spend a single cent of our small business' money and to make it on her own. Her hard work, tenacity, and will for success allowed her to trade sweat equity for her first commission cheque in her first week as a Network Marketer. Since the beginning of her journey in 2003, she has yet to miss a week of commission.

There is nothing stronger than the will of a driven woman. Such was the case of my mum. For five straight years my dad was extremely negative and closed off to the idea of Network Marketing, yet my mum force-fed him our company's products, and for those five years, he did the research into our company and the industry. During that time I had watched my mum go through adversity after adversity, rejection after rejection whilst looking after three shoe stores. She inspired me. There's no other way to describe it.

Fast forward to 2007. I didn't know it at the time, but the financial crisis was around the corner, my parents were constantly fighting and arguing over money and finances and everyone in the household was stressed. It was my 12th birthday and I was eagerly awaiting a birthday gift from my parents. I was hoping for the new Harry Potter book, but instead, they had bought me 'Rich Dad Poor Dad' by Robert Kiyosaki. It was this gift that changed my life and shifted my perspective on money and the world. This was my first exposure to personal development and financial education. They had bought me the book because one of their Network Marketing leaders had given them the book as homework for the week. I'm eternally grateful for that as it marked the beginning of my entrepreneurial journey.

It was during this period, the world started to collapse around my family, the global financial crisis hit, the e-commerce world started to grow rapidly, and my parents couldn't pivot their businesses fast enough. We ended up with over a million dollars of debt. Worse, we had a brand-new mortgage and a house full of unwanted inventory. It was as if the world was falling in around us in slow motion. I was desperately afraid my parents were going to get a divorce.

We were so short on money at one stage that my parents had to borrow hand-me-downs for my first day of high school and buying groceries was a struggle. With so much money locked away in all of the leftover stock at home, we struggled to pay bills. It got to the point where my parents borrowed money from *my* tiny little savings account, we had to pick out leftover produce from the produce bins at weekend markets just to get our vegetables for the week and stick to eating porridge because it was cheap. In all honesty, I never took it as eating from the trash at that time, I thought my parents were just smartly saving money, but in truth, it was because we didn't have enough.

I know this sounds like a sob story but it's simply the truth of our life. Sometimes life is hard, sometimes life is not fair, but it is what you make of it and as a family, we never gave up.

Even during this time of hardship, my mum's Network Marketing business had continued to pay her week after week even when our traditional business didn't. That in itself was enough for us to scrape by. My dad finally decided to make the pivot and with his back against the wall, he dove into Network Marketing with my mum. Finally, his mind opened, they began to rise through the ranks and build their team.

In Chinese we often say, if you work together as a couple you can turn dirt into gold and if you work together as a family you can turn gold into diamonds. And so they worked. They worked hard, meeting after meeting, presentation after presentation, they gave it their all. Eventually, they expanded their business globally. My dad went overseas to build up an organisation in Malaysia whilst my mum looked after my brother and me here in Australia.

It wasn't easy for my mum nor my dad. My mum had to take on the challenges of her business whilst juggling two adolescent teens going through their rebellious phase, my dad had to live alone away from his family to build his business overseas. I could see that it wasn't easy, so I wanted to remove as much stress off my parent's shoulders as possible. As soon as I turned the legal age of working in Australia, I went out to find a job. At 14, I worked hard, really hard. Whilst all my friends were going to tutoring or studying after school, I would go to work for a few hours to earn some money. It taught me a strong work ethic. I was hungry, not for food, but growth and knowledge.

From the age of 14, I worked in fruit shops, markets, retail stores, gyms, door-to-door sales, personal training, sports coaching, tutoring, labouring, the list goes on and on. Having the immigrant mentality ingrained into me, I looked out for all sorts of opportunities. I asked every boss I had ever worked for to take me under their wing and teach me everything they knew about business. I tried everything I could get my hands on and I wanted to be able to give back to my family. In most cases, I knew I wasn't the most talented, smartest, or the right age for the job, but I knew no one could outwork me. Watching my parent's struggles taught me to never be scared of hard work, and I knew I could outwork anyone. That drive and hunger helped me be the fastest and youngest promoted in almost all roles I have ever taken on.

It wasn't until university when I started to question my intentions with life and what I had wanted to achieve. I knew I wanted to be successful, but I hadn't decided on what path to take. I was exceptional in every job I had, yet I was always still broke, struggling to get by and unfulfilled. I would get bored every single time I hit my glass ceiling. I reflected on the book Rich Dad Poor Dad and I revisited the concept of trading time for money versus leverage. I had to get my priorities straight and I looked at what my parents were doing. At this stage, they had done relatively well in their Network Marketing business. They were travelling multiple times a year, going on incentive trips with their teams, had more freedom and were happier than before.

I started to question whether the traditional pathway that I had been taught to walk was correct. Sure, I would be more educated than my predecessors, but would I be more fulfilled and more successful?

I was going through the path that my parents picked out for me – I went to an academically elite high school, ranked in the top 10 schools in my state, Sydney Boys High School. I made it into a top tier university, the University of Sydney, to study science and potentially become a dietician or doctor. Even with all of these academic accomplishments, I just knew I wasn't on the right track. Why did I not see a future for myself that was financially or spiritually abundant?

I knew that building a successful business was the answer and that caused a huge conflict with the path I was taking. I was on the way to become skilled and very employable, but I had no faith that that would give me the life I was searching for. I searched for the perfect business for me, but with $10,000 in my savings account, my options were limited. Never did I expect the answer to be right at home. I had always thought that Network Marketing was for old, uneducated people, never did I think it was for a millennial. But I decided to do some research into it and to do it my way. I shadowed my parents and fell in love with the community, positivity and the opportunity to grow.

So I decided to join my parents' business. But as an ego-driven 19-year-old, I refused to listen to their advice. I was so ego-driven I told my parents that they were too old, and their methods were irrelevant to me. I was younger, smarter and faster, I would do things my way. They responded by giving me space to explore and more importantly the space to make mistakes. I worked hard, I tried to work things out myself, and I made tons of mistakes. Reflecting now, I could have skipped so many mistakes if I had just listened, but my method was working. I had built a small team of friends, we were making sales and we were growing.

At the end of my first year in business and university, my team and I were planning how to take our business to the next level. To my surprise, my best friend told me, "Allen, I don't think I can do this anymore. I'm not sure this is what I want. I'm out." This broke my heart, I tried to remain composed but deep down inside, it hurt. We were one year in together, we trained together, built our business together and learned together and then he quit on me. It didn't end there, later that week the rest of my team came to me one after another and told me the same thing. I was devastated. To further add salt to the wound, that same week, I received my university results for the term and I had failed 7 out of 10 courses accompanied by a Dean's letter warning me that I faced potential expulsion over my grades. This moment changed my life. I had a choice to make, either continue pushing forward, or I would lie down defeated and go back to the traditional life.

I made a hard decision. I decided to cut back on my Network Marketing business and take a break. But my parents always taught me to finish what I started; so, I intended to do just that. I took a break for almost three years to finish my university degree and prove to myself that I could get through hardship. The day I finished my degree I decided to get straight back into my business, and I promised myself this time it would be different.

I dropped my ego, I put my head down and I went to work. I drove hours to the office in our home city, I sat in training sessions where I could, I listened to personal development and read books in my spare time and I presented to anyone who would hear me out. I did that for a solid three months with no results, I put in 80-hour weeks every week to get my business up and running and I got back to back "NO's" and rejections daily. I went through over 50 no's in a row until I got my first customer and from that first customer, my business now spans globally.

My parents and I decided that we would split our operation and work as a family, I would focus primarily on an English market and they would focus on the Chinese market and just like that, when a family comes together and works together, we were able to turn gold into diamonds. It wasn't easy, but nothing in life ever is. You have to choose your battles and I had chosen this one, with the full intent of winning. I learnt many lessons in this business and even more about myself, who I am as a person and as a leader. This time around we chose to collaborate better, I designed and implemented systems, focused more on teaching skills and creating a stronger strategy for building a business online.

Now I predominantly build my business online through social media and my phone. I teach core business skills and help people develop a bulletproof mindset to become their most powerful and confident self. I would say Network Marketing has allowed me to become a better person.

But make no mistake, Network Marketing is not easy, it is simple. Network Marketing has allowed normal individuals like me and my parents to become valuable and fulfilled. We've been blessed to travel the world with our business, build it through our phones and the internet and I've been able to meet thousands of people, speak on global stages, work with amazing entrepreneurs, but most importantly it gave me a chance. It gave me a platform that allowed me to become the best me. This profession has given me and my family a chance to become extraordinary while achieving the freedom my parents chased after. We recently joined the Hall of Fame in our company and became Million Dollar Club Members (Earning over US$1,000,000 in commissions only).

I am grateful for our immigrant mentality. The ability to seek out and take opportunities from all sorts of directions, the delayed gratification of sacrificing now for a better tomorrow and the tenacity of fighting adversity head on have allowed us to build a better life. I'm sure that if you adapt some of these immigrant traits that you can make Network Marketing work for you. I hope that my story has inspired you to become the best you.

MOMENTUM MAKERS

1. YOUR FAMILY IS YOUR FOUNDATION: You will build the rest of your life with your family. Whether or not they are in business with you every day, they are in your business with you. Build a solid foundation in your closest relationships you will need it.

2. BE BOLD: You have to believe in yourself before others will follow your lead. Let go of any negative energy that would hold you back. Don't allow your subconscious to control your destiny. Let go and jump!

3. BUILD YOURSELF: You have to invest in your own development in order to grow your business. Life is about learning every day. Don't allow yourself to be complacent and stop growing.

MONA CHRISTENSEN

WISDOM WINS

I am a mature woman who was raised and still lives in Denmark. I grew up in a family with entrepreneurial parents; as a result, it was no surprise that I had the dream of succeeding with something of my own. I had good grades in school, and my teachers often told my parents that I could do much better if I put in the effort. But school did not interest me. I was a more creative child who enjoyed doing things and got bored just sitting down and listening or just doing what I was told. I really wanted to explore my creative sides more, and I did that during my younger years.

My parents had a successful business providing aluminum masts for sailboats, and I saw the passion, the hard work and the reward. I wanted for many years to build a business myself, but over and over I ran out of money and had to get a job.

One of my girlfriends had a shop and started telling me about some nutritional supplements and the system with Network Marketing. I must admit I really didn't understand it, but I signed up anyway. I never sold one single product or even used it myself. I became convinced that this Network Marketing thing didn't work or was just for certain people with very special talents or that it was only for people who were focused on money. Instead, for 6 years, I pursued a career in family counseling.

In one year, everything changed. I had just broken up with a boyfriend and then found out I was pregnant. This was not planned in any way, and I had to face the reality that I was going to be a single mother. At first, I was relieved that I had a job, which gave me maternity leave and social benefits, but then I realized my job was not going to change my working hours to adjust to my reality of being a single mom. I knew I would be out of a job as soon as the maternity leave ended. I felt I had no choice but to try and make a living as an independent therapist. While pregnant I started to prepare the business. I made a website, opened an office and so on. And I felt really good that I had my parents to help me make it all work.

But 10 days after I had given birth, my dear father had a stroke and was rushed to intensive care. He and my mother had been together for 46 years. As you could imagine, she was quite traumatized. I became fully focused on the immediate crisis of caring for my mother and father. My older brother was busy taking care of my parents' company, so all in all, we were really in a hard place as a family. Watching my dad go from highly productive to fully dependent helped me understand that my therapist business was not going to work. It was 100% dependent on my time. If I were sick or if clients cancelled I would have no money. At the same time, I could feel that listening to people's problems all day combined with my own problems was not healthy for me. I had to find another solution for income.

In one sense, I did not choose Network Marketing, it chose me. I had heard of residual income, and I was convinced that this was my only choice now and that I had to make the Network Marketing idea work. So I began to find out as much as I could about residual income, investing and Network Marketing. In just a few years I had worked hard and succeeded in creating a decent income with Network Marketing in combination with my hours working as a therapist.

Eventually, I found the company and product that suited me, and then things really to take off. I became the highest rank in Denmark with this company, and in 3 years, I was a top earner making a 6-figure income and continuing to rise.

The story is not about my success, however. The real story is about what

Network Marketing has provided me. Network Marketing has helped me live the life of my dreams. That's one of the tremendous values of Network Marketing. It is what you make it out to be. It can be tailored to fit your dreams as it did mine.

Over the course of my life, I have learned many things. Now, I'm in a position I did not realize I could be in so many years ago. I am helping others grow their business and make their impact – a true blessing. I am often asked, "How do you get to a place of success in Network Marketing?" I have settled on the following 10 critical lessons.

Learn from someone who has had the success you want. Spend time watching videos and going to trainings to learn. Take all the knowledge you can find and try it out. Network Marketing is a league of its own, and you need to learn skills from different areas like psychology, communication, marketing, sales, etc. If you are not coachable you will not be able to succeed.

Take full responsibility for your own business. Everyone is always starting with nothing and creating teams out of likeminded people. Yes, in Network Marketing we get a lot of help both in the way that we get to buy into a business that is made beforehand so we don´t have to reinvent the wheel and we get uplines that can help and teach us, BUT... You are the biggest factor in your own success. You can´t blame the products, your sponsor or anything or anyone else for not being successful. All the top earners I know have had times of losing teams, problems with products or even having a company shut down. They moved on, they took responsibility and built an even bigger level of success. No one knows what your journey will become, but I can almost promise you that it will not be success from start to finish. You will have to overcome challenges and prevail to become a top earner.

Be wise with your money. Network Marketing can make you a lot of money, but in the beginning, you need to invest a lot of time without getting big amounts of money. This is part of the learning process. Even professionals like lawyers do not make money while studying; so, be patient. Even when you start to earn money, don't make foolish decisions with it. You never know if something will change with your company or your team, so you can't rely on the money you get from your company.

Start to invest before you spend money on fun stuff or increasing your standard of living. You are fully financially free when you have several incomes that each could cover your monthly living expenses and not before that. So use some of the money you earn to invest in something long term. Being a wise investor will help you achieve full financial freedom long term. Imagine having an investment that very securely can pay your monthly bills with no work at all, and then having the income from your Network Marketing company for fun and building up other long-term investments. I have seen too many 6 and 7 figure income earners going bankrupt in a short time, because something happens to their team or their company, so be smart with your hard-earned money.

Go to events. It can both be generic events but also company events. This is where you learn to from the best in your company or the best in the industry. You also get to meet people who are just like you and hear their story and you will make friends that will support you even long distance. Everyone needs to fill up on energy, inspiration, and motivation once in a while, and events are where you will go to stock up on all that and build confidence in your opportunity. Not everyone who goes to an event will become a leader, but all leaders go to events.

Create new relationships all the time. Not just friends on Facebook, but friends that you can joke with and create million dollars relationships with. People who will after some time trust you and like you. If you can connect with people in an airport or in a café and create honest relations, then you will be a true networker. If you don't build new relations, you will have a hard time building your Network Marketing business.

Learn to present the business opportunity. Too many networkers love the products but suck at presenting the business opportunity and it will not create residual income. You must get to the point where you can present the business in your sleep. Practice makes perfect and this is the area that you need to practice.

Be a good person. Treating people with respect and care is crucial in this business. Your reputation is your network in this business. Don´t be vindictive. Don´t talk bad about other people. Don´t get arrogant. Don´t look down on others. Be polite. Forgive a lot. Your reputation is personal branding and you never know when you will meet the same person again and you don´t know who they know. Try not to argue, since this creates distance between you and the other person. A lot of times you just need to let it go to get peace of mind. Understand that what they do, is making sense to them although you might not understand it from your point of view. Your reputation is a part of your personal branding, and personal branding is important in this industry.

Be brave. Being brave means that you are a little afraid of doing it, but you do it anyway. This may seem like a simple concept; however, stepping into challenges is difficult. It takes bravery to believe in what you're doing enough to tell others it's what you do. You have to be bold about what you believe your business can become. When you start out, it will be an infant; but you cannot give up on the vision you see. Believe enough in what you're doing to challenge your inhibitions.

Surround yourself with likeminded people. Nothing can bring you down like being around people who don´t understand what you are doing or even talk bad about it. This can suck the enthusiasm right out of you, so if you are really serious about making it in this industry, you might have to get new peers. In the beginning, it might just be one or two people that you check in with to get inspiration, support and new energy, but eventually you will get a team of people who, together, create positive energy. This is so important since we all have to overcome obstacles but need moral support and cheering now and again.

Be patient. Building teams to the point where you can relax more takes time. A long time. You never know in this industry what happens next. Your best team leader might take 5 months off because of pregnancy. Another team leader might leave and take their team with them. Your company might change something significant or even close down forcing you to start over. Don´t give up. Keep going. Keep building teams and keep your head high. Some people get luckier than you. Keep going. Some people might surpass you. Keep going. Some people might leave you and talk bad about you. Keep going. If you are not in this industry for the long term, don´t expect results.

Go all in. Network Marketing is a lifestyle and you have to incorporate the actions you need to take into your daily routines. You have to be willing to put your Network Marketing business before many other things in your life. Some birthdays will not be as important as a meeting with a new rep. You have to learn about not just your own company but learn about the whole industry. Don´t be seduced by one company or one personality but be realistic and wise in your choices and your approaches. To be a professional you need to be educated and experienced as a professional. You need to be able to recognize true opportunities and hype. You need to be connected and stay informed. You need to be willing to give up some friends that will try to stop you from having success or who tell you that what you are trying to do is impossible.

Network Marketing has provided a real career for me. It helped take me from an unexpected, hard life start as a very young single mother caring for her parents to a place where I am blessed to experience a quality of life that provides time freedom, financial security and comfort. My hope for you is that it does the same.

MOMENTUM MAKERS

1. **THEY DON'T UNDERSTAND THE VALUE OF MONEY:** Be intentional with your money. Expect it to deliver a return for you. Spending money is when you will not get anything back for it. Investing money is when you expect to get something back. Make a decision to only spend money on things you need so that you continue to have money to grow your business and your life.

2. **THEY DON'T TAKE RESPONSIBILITY:** No one is going to grow your business for you. You must drive the success every day. Don't make excuses. If you're not getting the job done, be honest about it and change your habits.

3. **THEY DON'T PRACTICE:** People think building a business is easy. Selling a great product or service is just the first step. You have to practice your pitch and presentation. Don't take people's time for granted. Make sure when they show up, you show up.

NINA ALEXANDER
MAKE EVERYDAY COUNT

I grew up as the only child to entrepreneurial parents. My father had always had his own business and my mother was a passionate networker, who had been looking for 'the next big thing' for as long as I could remember.

18 months before she tragically passed away from cancer, my mother had become affiliated with a start-up Network Marketing company in the UK. I will never forget the phone call I received from the owner of the company shortly after she died. He said 'Nina, you are your mum's only child and she would want you to benefit from her hard work. The clients she introduced to our product are still buying it, and that commission is all yours, provided they continue to purchase. She was doing it all for you anyway." I do not know of many industries that offer this concept and it is, in my opinion, one of Network Marketing's greatest assets.

I was 28 when my mother died. I was single and I rented a house with my girlfriends. I was earning a generous salary thanks to my successful career in advertising, but I was already experiencing 'burn out'. I had subsequently decided many years before that I did not want to work for a boss, I no longer wanted to commute and I definitely did not want to spend the next 50 years of my life stuck in an office, restricted to 25 days of holiday per year. I wanted to live my best life on my terms. Losing my mum was a massive reinforcement that life is short. We all have just one chance to make our lives the best they can possibly be. This powerful realisation triggered me to resign from my highflying corporate career, never to return.

I was a broken woman, suffering from immeasurable grief and loss, and I had an overwhelming urge to run away. Looking back, this was a transformational decision that positively impacted both my mind-set and my future career path. I fled to South East Asia where I embarked upon a healing journey for my soul. I spent time in retreats and wellness centres and even became a Reiki Master.

When I returned to the UK, I continued my journey of self-discovery and trained in Anatomy and Physiology, beauty, make up and holistic therapy. I became confident that this was the path to enable me to have a career that I loved and most crucially, on my terms. I built a small business as a therapist. Pretty soon, I had regular clients and during my first year of business, I met the man who would become my husband a year later. We had two baby boys, 18 months apart and I became pregnant with a third son soon after.

Becoming a mother myself forced me to reduce my number of clients. This left my husband with the financial pressure of paying the bills. We soon realised that we needed to move to a bigger house to accommodate our ever-growing family and, for the first time, I questioned whether I was destined to go back into advertising in order to earn a decent income to help support my family.

As if by a twist of fate, during that time in 2013, I was approached to join a Network Marketing Company in the health, wellness and beauty industry. I was truly impressed with the quality of the products and agreed to become an independent consultant. However, I was cautious as to how on earth I would fit this business into my busy life as a mother of young children.

Despite this hesitation, I had an overwhelming gut instinct that this brand and business opportunity was going to transform my life and I became truly passionate about sharing both the products and the business. At the same time, we had our third child (which meant we had 3 children all under the age of 3 years old) and moved to a larger home. It would have been easy to put my new business on hold with the chaos of that year, but isn't life always crazy busy these days? I followed the advice from my mentors and quit watching reality TV! This created an extra 7 hours per week, which I devoted solely to growing my business. I believed that with time and consistent effort, I could build up a successful business. After I started selling products and developing a team that sells products, I was starting to earn commissions. My sales continued to grow monthly and my commission cheque reflected this. This industry was the best-kept secret in the world in my opinion!

Network Marketing is a genius, yet very simple business model that is often misidentified in the world of business. Put simply, all I was doing was selling products to end consumers. People sometimes wonder what the "catch" is with Network Marketing… it sounds too good to be true. There really isn't a catch, but there is a stipulation and that is this - you MUST have a strong work ethic. There is a strong commonality between the forerunning leaders in my team and that is they work hard and smart and they don't quit when the going gets tough. One of the most unfortunate myths of this industry is that it is not a viable business model because only a few succeed and get to the top of the organisation. The top performers in any organisation, team or community are those that persevere and have an incredible work ethic. I have learned in my business that too many people quit before they have even got started. So many will have a knockback early on and they will decide that this industry is not for them, or in some cases believe and tell others that Network Marketing doesn't work. I perceive this belief to be as futile as believing that a Gym "doesn't work" because so many people join in January and quit in February. This same analogy can be applied to the reality that the people that don't quit Network Marketing are the individuals that can thrive and reach the top.

This business allows me to work from anywhere I desire and I book my diary around my life, my family and my daily commitments including the gym. I have never missed a child's birthday or a school nativity play, and I take my children to and from school every day. Some days, if I fancy taking a day off to have a bit of "me time", I will. I can choose to get my nails done, have a massage or have lunch with a friend whenever I wish because I am my own boss. I have the opportunity to earn incentive trips and rewards when I achieve certain sales goals, and I get to experience the joy of mentoring my team and helping them reach their goals.

So, you may be reading this and thinking, well this all sounds great but what did you actually do to achieve this? Well, I was loud and I was proud! I got out there and shared the products and the business opportunity with a LOT of people. I worked hard to lose my ego and not worry about what people thought of me by focusing on the end result. There was a bigger picture than the short-term reality of someone with a closed mind rolling their eyes that I had joined a cult! I had a family to feed and a bad-ass business to build. I reasoned that if others had succeeded in Network Marketing, then it could be done.

If they could do it, why not me?

I was already a big believer in the power of positive thinking and I regularly wrote affirmations that stated the things that I wanted to attract into my life. I got very busy writing affirmations for my new business venture. I wrote down things like how many people I wanted in my team by the end of my first year and when I wanted to reach the first level of management by. After my first year, I was excited to reflect back that I had achieved every single goal I had written!

I lay awake for nights on end with extreme excitement, nerves, determination and fear – all at once! I contacted my past and present network and invited them to presentations where I would share the products and the business opportunity. If they couldn't make it, I offered to meet with them personally and, looking back, I think the fact that my passion and belief in the company was so strong, they realised I was doing this properly and many of those initial friends jumped in. Ironically, the first person to join my business was the first person to quit, yet I am eternally grateful to her for getting my team up and running and for being the first person to believe in me as a mentor.

I had never had any previous experience or training as a business coach or mentor but the more my team grew and the more books I read about leadership, the more comfortable I felt in this role.

There are many different types of leaders and I would describe my leadership style as caring, nurturing, uplifting and fun. It is important for you to realise that any style of personality works in this industry. I work alongside people from all different backgrounds and belief systems. This is an opportunity for ANYONE to build a successful business, with or without educational qualifications. However, in my opinion, there is an identifiable blueprint of qualities it takes to be a successful Network Marketing Leader.

Here are the top 5 qualities, alongside a good work ethic as I have already mentioned, that I believe it takes to succeed in this industry:

1. Consistency: Taking intentional, daily actions is KEY

2. Knowledge is POWER: You must know your brand and industry

3. Influence & Likeability: People work with people they know AND like

4. Belief: You must maintain a self-belief and an unwavering BELIEF in the path you have chosen

5. Drive and Determination: You must push through the barriers that will want to keep you from success

When I started my business in 2013, the industry was slightly different in the sense that social marketing hadn't really taken off. I was communicating with my team through email and messaging, which seems archaic now. Social media platforms have revolutionised our industry. The vast majority of my business now is done via Facebook, Instagram, WhatsApp, and Zoom. My team members are accustomed to my live motivational videos – they have become my ultimate communication tool. I have a global business with teams in many different countries and I can coach and mentor them from the comfort of my own home. This is so perfect for me and many members of my team who have young children. If you ever see me on a coaching call, I may have my lipstick and a nice top on, but underneath I will be wearing pajama bottoms and slippers! I have lost count of the number of times one of my children has walked in naked or hungry when I have been on a video call, but it all adds to the reality of this business! Yes, I am a successful businesswoman but first and foremost, I am a mother. My children will always take priority.

When I reached the top level of management within the company, the biggest emotion I experienced at reaching the top level was relief. Relief that I had stuck it out. Relief that I had said yes. This achievement was also within the year that our 4th child was born – a beautiful baby girl arrived to complete our family of 6. In short, if I can do this, I believe ANYONE can too!

There are hundreds of reasons why I am completely in love with this industry, but here are my top 10 favourite things:

1. The people I have met, the friendships I have been blessed with and the belly laughs we have had. Thank you.

2. The business opportunity I have created for my family

3. The flexibility of being my own boss

4. Receiving the platform to serve, empower and inspire many people

5. Being fully present for my children and taking them to school everyday

6. Having no commute and working from any destination I wish

7. Witnessing lives transforming and the opportunity to give back

8. The positive community of like-minded people I am surrounded by

9. The opportunity to earn sales incentive trips to different countries

10. The personal development and confidence growth

The sense of gratitude I have for starting a Network Marketing business has never been more powerful than in recent times when I sustained a badly broken finger in a sports injury that resulted in surgery and a 3-4 month estimated full recovery. I could not use my dominant hand for many weeks and I could not drive, cook or do any household chores. As a mother of 4 children, this was very debilitating. If I didn't have my Network Marketing business, this would have had a devastating impact on our family because if I was reliant on just my make-up and beauty business, I would not have been able to do any clients whatsoever. On the contrary, my Network Marketing business has been unaffected because my clients and my team's clients continue to purchase products online. Everyone needs a Plan B income because otherwise what happens if someone in your house unexpectedly stops earning money? Network Marketing can empower ordinary hard-working people to live a different way of life.

My mother was always searching for the "next big thing" when she stumbled across Network Marketing. Even though she didn't live long enough to create a huge legacy, her gift was returned to me, years later, wrapped up in a business opportunity partnered with an incredible brand. Believe me when I say, this industry has the true potential to transform your life and it can allow you to indulge in your biggest dreams. I will always be truly thankful…both for the future potential that is still to unfold and for the magical memories I have already cherished.

MOMENTUM MAKERS

1. **CONSISTENCY ALWAYS MATTERS:** How many times do you need to hear something before you do something about it? We all have constant streams of noise in our life competing for every part of us, not just our time. People you know are suffering the same circumstances. Further, people do not attach themselves to things they do not have confidence in. You must be consistent to break through the noise in other people's lives AND you must be consistent for them to have confidence you are serious about what you're doing.

2. **MAXIMIZE EVERY OPPORTUNITY:** Every day you have hundreds of opportunities around you to shape people's lives and build your success. You cannot influence someone with whom you have no relationship. Maximize your relationships to foster your growth.

3. **DETERMINATION DRIVES SUCCESS:** "Never give up" can seem cliché; but it is the thing that propels you forward. It busts through the mountains in your life that would otherwise keep you from reaching your goals. Don't let roadblocks keep you from your dream.

HILARI & JUSTIN COURTNEY

ITS ABOUT YOUR TEAM, NOT YOU

So, let us not grow weary of doing good,
for at just the right time we will reap a harvest of blessing,
IF we don't give up.
Galatians 6:9

Wouldn't it be amazing if every day we could wake up fulfilled? What if every night when our heads hit the pillow, we felt like we made a difference? This ideal place is far from where we were when our journey began 19 years ago, before we were introduced to the profession of Network Marketing.

I had just graduated from college and had a corporate career anyone would want, but I would go home every night completely unfulfilled. I remember saying to my fiancé, now husband, "God has to have more for me than this. I really feel like I'm not making an impact for anyone. I have so many talents that I'm not even utilizing." We both grew up in the world of, go to college, get a degree and go to work for someone else forever! So his response was, "honey this is what adults do, they go to jobs every day, whether they like them or not." That didn't resonate well; I knew there was more for us.

Fast forward a couple of months and a friend of mine invited me to a Network Marketing presentation. I remember watching and thinking, this lady is no different from me. I could totally do this, and I could help other people. At that point, I began to dream of all the possibilities.

- What if I didn't have to work within these four walls that seemed to suffocate me?
- What if I could set my own hours and have time freedom?
- What if Justin and I could have kids and actually be present in their lives?
- What if we could help others have the same incredible opportunity?

And that, friends, is where our Network Marketing journey began. I will be the first to tell you this industry isn't perfect, but it is better than anything else we've ever seen. It has its ups and downs and, when people are starting out, that is something that I always make very clear. Be prepared to have a great day and the next day, your lifelong friend will return their products! It's part of the landscape of our incredible industry. The lesson is that if you are consistent, your new lows become your old highs, and your new highs are where you've never been before.

When I was introduced to the company that my husband and I have now been a part of for the last 14 years, I knew immediately this was our forever home. If you're looking right now, find a company that fits *your* values, one that aligns with what *you* personally believe in. We were so blessed to find a company that was all about vision and impact and making a positive difference in the lives of others. That was and still is exactly what we are about!

I clearly remember coming home from that event and being what I lovingly call "ignorance on fire". I shared with everybody that I possibly could. I truly believed that if they could see the vision I saw, their life would be forever changed. Now I just had to convince the other person living in our home! Because of past experiences in the industry, my husband was not on board. I find this to be very common in Network Marketing; one spouse is all in and the other is typically not so sure. If you've caught the vision but at first you don't have the full support of your spouse or significant other, it will be all right. I promise. Personally, I knew this was going to change my family's life and so I went for it. About a year later, my husband got on board and it's been such a blessing. We've been able to work our business together now for over 14 years and it's been incredible. My experience has shown me that if you stay consistent and committed, your residual income will grow, and your spouse will catch the vision! Remember new things can be intimidating!

The freedom we've gained through this journey has allowed us to both be at home with our four children, ages 12, 10, 6, and 5. Trust me, that is a full-time job in itself! Our children have always been our reason to attack this business model, never our excuse not to pursue it. We get to be with them as much as we want; field trips, classroom parties, we are always there. We have the time freedom to go to the lake for a month every summer and the memories we make will last forever. Our consistent work allows us to live in a small farming community in the middle of the country. It is so beyond peaceful, no rushing. This opportunity has allowed us to give more than we ever imagined possible. That's what life is really about!

We have enjoyed so much success! But, for us, passing that success onto others is really what it is all about. Our core learnings drive that success. Attaining our goals in the business has been the product of 5 key principles:

Invest in Others: Our number one priority is investing in our people. They are the lifeblood of our business. In our opinion, nothing should come above this. If you're in this business to serve people, you'll have more success than you could ever imagine. History shows us that the world's greatest leaders were the people who had a servant's heart and mentality. This business is all about helping others. We truly love our team. We pour our time and energy into them. I would encourage you to get to know your people and genuinely care about them. You need to know why they're doing this and how this could change their lives. Know their family, know their children's names, know the color of their living room carpet. Your greatest investment should be in your people.

Strategic & Intentional Community: We focus on creating the community we desire. If there is nothing going on in your geographical region, you must take initiative and create it yourself. We live in a rural community that is 60 miles from a city. We have never used that as an excuse. When we began, there were no meetings close to us, so we started a weekly wellness night. This was an opportunity for us and our team to bring guests and to grow! We would drive over 30 miles each way. This local meeting gave us the change to passionately share why we love this industry. Yes, you can now do so many things online, but we believe there is still nothing like being belly to belly. Just last fall we drove 6 hours to a team member's home in rural Wisconsin. She and her husband are now unstoppable!

Iron Sharpens Iron: We 100% believe Proverbs 27:17 when it says, "Iron sharpens iron as one person sharpens another" and helps people become the best leaders they can be. We run incentives and put them on teams. We have found this verse to be so applicable to our business. We create challenges that encourage positive competition.

The Piñata Mindset: We have adopted Alisa Keeton's, "Piñata Mindset". The Piñata Mindset is to have the abundance mindset of children. Think about a child's birthday party. It doesn't matter who breaks the pinata open, ALL the children get the candy. In this business, it is so easy to compare. And we know how that goes, it steals our joy. Instead, we decided that when someone gets an enrollment or advances in the company, we will celebrate their success with them. Knowing that if we just stay the course, our piñata will soon burst open. The team loved this so much they bought piñatas and have them up in their home offices!

Authentic Leadership: We have always done our best to lead from the front. What I mean by that is we are always "doing the do". We never want to tell our team to do something that we haven't done. If the company offers a promotion, we go for it. We are in the trenches with our team. We encourage them that we will do it together and we lock arms with them. One of our key strategies is to be as consistent as possible. We truly believe that in every area of life, whoever is consistent the longest wins.

Friends, success is intentional. When I was young, I was a dreamer. Now that I'm older and wiser, I'm still a dreamer but I have a plan! Success doesn't just happen to people. It takes preparation and consistently working on the fundamentals. You must know your goals and have a clear direction. You must know the next level and the steps that will get you there. It is a daily decision to take action. You must decide not to go alone, as real success is when your team succeeds right alongside you.

Lastly, we want to speak to you individually and tell you that you are incredible. God gave you talents that he did not give me or your spouse or your friends; they are innately yours. Live your life fully so that you can fully impact others. We know there are people who are praying for an answer to their health challenges, praying for an answer to their finances and praying for an answer to their lack of time freedom. We have the answer - Network Marketing is a better way. We challenge you to be good stewards of your talents because you never know who needs you to be brave and go first.

We promise that all of the ups and downs of this industry, all the sleepless nights, all the sweat and meetings when no one shows up will be totally worth it. For my husband and me, this has been a transformational experience; we are better versions of ourselves than when we began. I always say, "this is a personal growth journey with a paycheck attached". If you will just simply be consistent and stay true to your authentic self, you will be able to leave a legacy, not only for your family, but a legacy for thousands of other families as well. Be clear on your vision and your mission and go out and set others free!

MOMENTUM MAKERS

1. **BIRDS OF A FEATHER:** As mentioned, your time is your most precious commodity. You need to be highly strategic with it. They say that you will become the type of person that is the type of person you spend time with. You will either be built up or torn down by the people you are around. You will either be the person they mimic or you will mimic them. Be intentional in constructing your circles of relationship.

2. **IT'S NOT ALL ABOUT YOU:** Relationships are an exchange. They are bi-directional. Whether you are meeting someone for the first time or you have known them a lifetime. Everyone wants to walk away from an encounter with you feeling good about themself. Make a commitment to take them on a journey in every exchange to a better place. Even if you don't have the wisdom to improve their particular circumstance, you do have the encouragement to cheer them on.

3. **BE AUTHENTIC:** People are attracted to things they trust. The more authentic you are in your relationships, the more relationships you will have. In every conversation you walk away from, you need to ask yourself, "What did I learn about them?" and "What did they learn about me?" Make your meetings with other people count.

PILLE KAPETANAKIS

THE ONE QUESTION THAT CHANGED EVERYTHING

This early July morning I felt compelled to make myself an awesome cup of coffee and head out to the patio with my laptop and write you a story about how one question changed my life.

Keep reading....

I made the decision to leave the corporate world behind and work from home about 7 years ago. First, as an owner of a traditional business – importing and distributing eyewear from France ...

We all know that working for someone else means getting dressed, having to show up every day, having some sort of a false sense of security, having a more or less defined monthly paycheck (you can only make up to a certain amount), and a glass ceiling (can't out promote your boss!). That kind of environment was something that I called my job for many years. You might be able to relate to it.

I had always loved the idea of not having a boss and working for myself, so the decision to start our own business out of our home using my years of experience in the optical industry was born. We started a national eyewear import/distribution business in Canada that I was going to run while my husband continued his job away from home as a captain.

We found an amazing funky handmade product line from France to work with, invested nearly 6 figures into inventory and startup costs, and felt that this was going to be it. Jackpot. It seemed like an ideal situation at the time and we were excited about saving on overhead costs by transforming our garage into the headquarters of this venture. I stayed up late nights for months on end, trying to get things off the ground. Entering inventory, converting Euros to Canadian dollars - figuring out perfect pricing formulas, assembling sample kits for sales reps, drafting contracts for accounts and sales reps, negotiating commissions…. I was the jack of all trades in the beginning, and saving where we could was a big deal.

Those times were a mix of extreme excitement (can't believe we started a business; we will make so much money!!) and doubt (did we do the right thing?).

Fast forward, we saw the worst ups and downs – being affected by the economy, our customer accounts shutting down or downsizing, sales reps being hired only to be quit soon after - me picking up the slack by flying all over the country to keep our accounts serviced and happy; accounts not paying their bills on time or not at all. Yes, we got to go to court to fight them! Yikes!

On top of it all, dealing with advertising, the daily shipping of orders, being on the phone with accounts (while juggling to find a quiet spot to speak while our kids were running around in the background), order entries and invoicing, accounts payable/receivable, bookkeeping and anything else daily operations entails made our lives crazy. Can you sense overwhelm and stress?

Needless to say, we found that it is hard to run a traditional business – it is not all butterflies and sunshine. I had hoped this would allow us to have more time freedom so we could travel more. Was I ever wrong! We were literally married to the business and the business was running our lives. We could not take any time off at all.

In fact, it used to drive me crazy when people said to me that it must be so nice and easy because you get to work from home. Somehow, they had this idea that owning a business is easy and involves endless coffee breaks and fun.

No.

It took a ton of self-discipline, scheduling, and figuring out how to do this all while taking care of kids. It was a huge responsibility because I had to stay on top of most of this by myself, even when some of the tasks were outsourced, because my husband was working to make sure we had some semblance of consistency.

Having lived the corporate world employee and traditional business owner's life, having experienced the pros and cons of both, stumbling across Network Marketing has been quite a refreshing breath of air.

I chose to get involved with my current company in August 2015, after being cold prospected on social media. I had no idea what I was doing and did not have any proper experience or training in this business model at all.

I remember I briefly complained to my husband that I had been prospected for this company on social media and how I was not interested, and asked him what I should tell the lady as the follow-ups kept coming (insert eye roll). He thought I should give it a try. Him, who would never do this kind of a business in a million years! What??

He encouraged me to join because he had noticed I was unhappy with what I was doing. He was right, but there was no way someone like me could actually succeed in Network Marketing. That was my limiting belief back then. And a darn good excuse, don't you think?

As you can see, I was already so insanely busy, I was not looking to add anything else to my plate. I could barely get enough sleep between running the distribution business and running after the kids!

But one day when I was chatting with a friend about the reality of our crazy life, she asked me: **"wow, so how long will you have to do all this** for?"

That question right there. It changed **everything.**

Really! How long was I going to have to run like a hamster in a wheel if I kept doing what I was doing? What a scary thought!

I realized that unless I made a change, this was going to be my life for many long years to come. The whole home business idea was born from the desire to be my own boss, have lots of time and financial freedom – something that had not happened 5 years into the venture, and at the rate, was not going to happen any time soon. It took us 3 years alone to break even! Barely! And I was exhausted!

When I joined Network Marketing as a sideline, I was somewhat skeptical and I naturally tried to relate this business model to our eyewear business, thinking it will be the same (oh how wrong was I!).

Having seen and worked in various environments, I do have experience and expertise in the field I was trained in, and I like to weigh my business decisions carefully – I was not going to get involved in anything that would hurt my reputation that I had spent years building.

Despite the number of people around me being negative Nellies and telling me, "this will not work" (insert auntie Bonnie's failed MLM story from 1980's and a story about uncle Joe's high pressure sales tactics that scared the whole town away), some people even unfriending me after finding out what I was doing, I decided to go all in and give it a really good, serious try.

I was going to follow the system and do whatever they told me I should do.

I figured the worst that could happen is me having a $400 tax deduction - the cost of the product pack I had bought for myself. I was mentally ready to do what it takes to make a change and start making the money our family deserves and get my life back.

It's amazing what one little decision can do.

What I have found over the last 4 years, is that this is, hands down, the best business model I have ever come across.

Why? Let me crack open the door just a little, so you can see….

First of all, I was able to start a business with a very tiny investment – $400 (four hundred. Not four thousand) – nothing like our other business which was close to 6 digits to get up and running. Sounds appealing? It sure did to me!

Next – it has been risk free. I have not had to put my family's savings on the line to start, and no investment in inventory that may or may not sell. The accounting and shipping is taken care of for me, and I don't have to worry about unpaid accounts that affect the cash flow.

My favorite part is being able to travel and get my income producing activities done from anywhere - whether it's 35,000 feet up in the air, beaches in warm places, or while sitting on the sidelines at my kids' taekwondo class or my own backyard oasis.

I made it to a 6-figure yearly income in my year 2 and it's only grown from there.

I was able to kiss the eye care industry goodbye after just 5 months in Network Marketing because it surpassed my monthly salary at that point. You can't imagine the relief I felt when we shut down our eyewear company - it was like taking off a backpack filled with bricks. I could finally breathe again!

Another massive positive in this industry is all the friends I have made along the way. I'm naturally an introvert, and never had a lot of friends - especially after leaving Estonia where I was born and raised, and moving to Canada. I always found myself making "work friends" who came and went as I was changing jobs. But I had very few real lifelong meaningful friendships.

That all has changed - I'm surrounded by a happy supportive family every single day - whether virtually or in person and that is one thing I value so much. I've evolved into a leader that people want to work with and see value in, and that is something that drives me to serve more people on a larger scale, globally.

It's pretty common on everyday jobs to see people competing for that manager's or supervisor's position, stepping on each other and trying to prove why they deserve to be the next rockstar. There's that ladder and only one person can get to the top and the race is on!

Network Marketing is so different - we empower each other to be the best version of ourselves, we want to be and do better as humans, and offer help and support to those around us. It's like we are a different breed. I have been actually accused of being "too happy" and "fake happy" and told that this cannot be real. How hilarious is that?! I guess it can be so foreign for those not involved in this industry, to realize that this is life, this is real, we are genuinely happy with the life we have created, and that they can be a part of it too.

How did I not "get it" years ago? Why didn't anyone tell me what it's really like? Why didn't anyone shine a ray of hope on me that there is a better way, show me how I too can build a large team and have a residual income stream that outperforms my traditional business income from early on? Why didn't anyone feel that I was *worthy enough to be prospected* much sooner than that?

So. Many. Questions.

At this point, you're probably wondering how I get the word out and if I bug my friends and family to make money in this. Well, I'm glad you are wondering, because I was too, before I really understood what's involved. My short answer is no, I do not bother my friends or family. And no, I don't do home parties, because this particular business is not built around a party plan. I also don't fill my friends' social media feed with endless spam about my company – in fact, it may take you a bit of time to figure out what is it that I even do.

There are very natural, pressure-free ways to introduce your business and products to people. I don't consider myself a salesperson at all, I really **do not like selling** anything to anyone. But what I do love is helping people solve problems, whether it is in the financial department or something my products can help them with.

I literally feel like my world has changed so much and is still changing right in front of my eyes.

I'm forever grateful for having been introduced to Network Marketing - and can't imagine where I'd be today if I hadn't taken the leap. I keep that in mind when I offer my opportunity to others - you just never know who has been praying for something like this, or needs this and doesn't even know it - just like I was 4 years ago.

MOMENTUM MAKERS

1. Start working before you know everything - when you run into questions - hop on a 3-way call or a 3-way messenger chat with your upline. It's better to be ignorance on fire than knowledge on ice (I have no idea who said it, but they said it so well).

2. Being coachable and not trying to re-invent the wheel. Work the system that is in place and that is working for others in your chosen company.

3. Consistency. Setting weekly and daily action goals. You can control how many people you prospect and follow up with, so focus on that over a long period of time. Some say to give it a year, some say 5 years. I say give it 2 years of consistent action and you will see results.

4. Focus on what your product or business DOES, not what it IS. Sell people on the benefit, not the ingredients or comp plan.

5. It's not about you; it's about them. Leave your ego behind and focus on helping others. How can you serve them? When you help enough people, your success is inevitable.

6. Do it despite the obstacles that get thrown your way.

7. Do it until you get the desired results.

8. The only way you will not succeed is when you give up.

9. As a leader, keep focusing on your personal business and avoid management mode at all costs. It will catch up to you.

10. Never compare yourself to others. Put your blinders on and focus on YOUR goals and YOUR business.

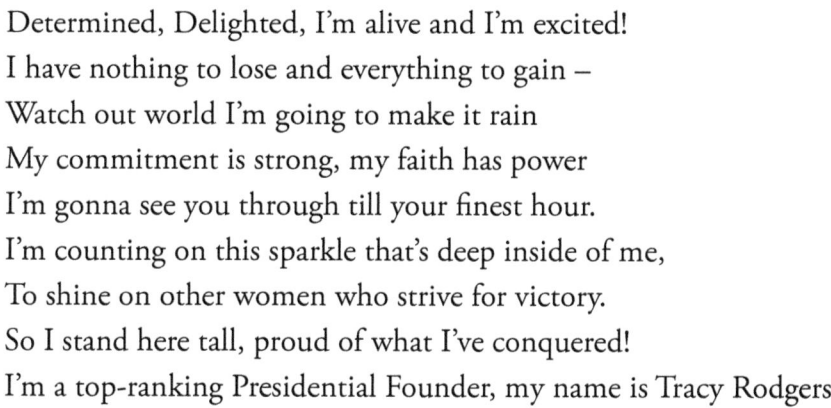

TRACY RODGERS

HOW BAD DO YOU WANT IT?

(your results are dependent on you)

Determined, Delighted, I'm alive and I'm excited!
I have nothing to lose and everything to gain –
Watch out world I'm going to make it rain
My commitment is strong, my faith has power
I'm gonna see you through till your finest hour.
I'm counting on this sparkle that's deep inside of me,
To shine on other women who strive for victory.
So I stand here tall, proud of what I've conquered!
I'm a top-ranking Presidential Founder, my name is Tracy Rodgers

This is my daily affirmation that I have recited every day for two and a half years. But this is not where my story began. Let's start at the beginning.

I began my Network Marketing career 33 years ago. I started because I was a single mom with 4 kids, and I needed to be able to stay home with them during the day. It was easy to get a sitter for a couple of hours while I did parties at night making this my only alternative to daycare because of the astronomical costs.

Over the years I've reached a certain level of success, but I never made it to the top level of a company with their compensation plan. I was quick to blame someone else for MY lack of success making it easy for me to start my search for a new company. My reasonings varied between: I felt the product was too expensive; I had an up-line who didn't support me; I didn't see eye to eye with the company values or whatever excuse I could find to justify my "reasons" for joining another company.

As I look back, I realized that I never took responsibility or ownership for not reaching that level of success I desired. The reality is if I had applied to my business what I knew then, I would have been where I am right now. I knew what needed to be done to be successful but knowing what to do and actually doing it are two different things. That was the biggest downfall for me – I knew what it took to do this business. I knew what it took to be a multi-million-dollar team, but I didn't apply it with consistency and action.

After being in the industry for 18 years, I decided that the Network Marketing corporate job was the route I wanted to go. I loved being able to teach women how to be successful with their business. I loved working with different women and companies giving me a lot of experience working with different personalities and how to be professional on a whole different level. When you are corporate you can't do the things that you would as a volunteer leader because you're being paid.

After a while, I realized that I was selling myself short because even though I was working corporate in a direct selling environment, I wasn't in direct sales myself and I really wanted the time freedom and the financial freedom that direct sales provide. After my last corporate Network Marketing job closed its doors and went retail, I decided to take a break from the Network Marketing industry.

My rags to riches journey actually started when I was working a j-o-b for the ferry system as a cook. I had taken a break from corporate training and was re-evaluating my life to find out what I wanted to be when I grew up. This is when things in my life started to spiral out of control. Life can throw you a curveball and it had certainly thrown me one. I found myself with medical and personal financial issues, working a slightly over minimum wage job, and my personal life was going downhill. After months of treading water, I ended up packing my car with four boxes and my dog.

I had lost everything, my home, my stability, my stuff, my security. Let me tell you, if you don't have six months of your income in savings, you are six months away from being homeless as I found out the hard way. Here I was with a few boxes and my dog – I can't tell you how hard this hit me – I was homeless.

People knew that it was bad for me. I live on an island. People knew that I was in a bad condition, but they didn't know how bad. On social media, especially with Facebook, we don't let people know the real details. Due to our pride and our community, we'll let people see a certain side of us, but not always the worst side or situation of us. Even though people knew that I was going through a really hard time and I had lost everything, people didn't realize things had gotten so bad that I was homeless.

People had been stepping up to help with their generosity however they could. But after a while, the well dries up, the road comes to an end, and I found myself on my own. Here I was working a full-time job and I lost everything. Being homeless can happen to hard-working people. After about a week I decided to go knock on my mom's door. I'm just going to say, "Mom, hey look, it's worse than you think, and I've lost everything. But if I can stay here for just a little while and get back on my feet, I'll contribute what I can for rent. I just need someplace to take shelter." And of course, my mom let me in because she's my mom, and she didn't realize how bad it was.

I was happily working on the ferry out of the San Juan Islands in Washington - It was beautiful. After about a month being at my mom's, I heard about this new company that was going to be launching. I looked into it and I knew that this was the one for me. I knew! I saw the vision! I believed in it! I knew that if I really sat down and applied myself, do what I needed to do and what I had taught other people to do for years, that this would be my opportunity to change my life!

I made a commitment that if I was going to do this, I was going to give it my all because it was my last shot. How much worse can it be when you're 56 years old, you've been homeless and you're living with you mom? I was committed to doing what I needed to do to make it a success! I decided I was going to make personal development a priority in my life and in my business. I said to myself, "Trace, you're going to add personal development to your life and you're going to take it to a whole new steroid level!"

That's when I started saying my affirmation (written above) twice a day when I walked my dog. I would recite my affirmation over and over to the point where the neighbors knew it by heart! I said it on my breaks as I walked around on the ferry. I recited my affirmation every day because that's what I was going to be! That's what my vision was! I needed to hear that affirmation for myself. As I was building my team and my business, I poured myself into personal development.

A month after our company launched, I was introduced to Rob Sperry's book, *The Game of Networking*. I was reading that all day and night. I went from one personal development book to a different personal development book. I needed to put the positive inside my brain while I was building my business because the world is very negative, and it can get you down.

I've discovered why personal development needs to be your biggest priority – because it changes our mindset, what we believe and it gives us verbiage, ideas and promotes our thinking towards success in our business. That's the biggest thing I did differently this time. I immersed myself with personal development. I literally went to sleep every night listening to Rob Sperry or John C. Maxwell or Ray Higdon, or any other great networking examples. It's the last thing that I wanted to hear, as I was falling asleep.

When people ask me, "what's the one thing that contributed to your success?" My answer is always "Because I made a commitment to personal development." When you're feeding your brain by reading or listening to personal development during the day and as you're falling asleep, it does change your mind. That's what helped me to stay focused enough to build my business. After four months of launching, I was able to quit my job on the ferry and do this full time!

This business is more than just about personal and financial gain. I saw the vision of what could be for my life and finances; but more importantly, I saw the vision of what it could do for other people. Within two years my team has grown to 18,000 people and I've been able to do things for other people, my family, and charities that are dear to my heart that I could never do before.

I took my mom at 77 years old on an inside passage cruise to Alaska. That was a dream come true for her! It was on her bucket list. My daughter who grew up in direct sales and wanted nothing to do with it had seen the success that I was having in a short amount of time. She joined and two years later she's one of the top 1% of the company for leaders and went from low-income housing to buying a brand-new home in two years!

This is what this industry can do! It's not just about us, it's for other people. I'm so blessed that I am able to do the things I'm doing and I'm so blessed that I said yes because so many other people have said yes as well!

As Rob Sperry says, "Die with memories, not with dreams." That's what I'm working on now to bless enough people and blessing my family and my grandchildren that I'm going to die with memories and not many dreams!

MOMENTUM MAKERS

1. **CIRCUMSTANCES DO NOT DETERMINE YOUR SUCCESS:** Stop believing lies that you cannot make it because you have not made it. Circumstances only help define the greatness of your success. The worse the shape you are in when you get started only helps to create the greatness of your story overcoming it.

2. **DEVELOP YOURSELF TO DEVELOP YOUR BUSINESS:** Wanting to improve your life requires improvements. You must be honest with yourself about what needs improvement AND be willing to make the changes required to improve.

3. **LET YOUR DREAMS DRIVE YOUR SUCCESS:** Every ambition begins with a dream. Yours should be written down. A dream is not an inspirational statement or a single attribute. "Being Rich" is not a dream. It is an attribute of a dream. Dreams should be detailed enough that someone could take your description and paint a picture of it.

JORDAN ADLER

HOW TO FLY IN LIFE AND IN BUSINESS

From as long as I can remember, I dreamt I could fly. Even as a 6-year-old, I remember walking into my backyard in the south suburbs of Chicago, spreading my arms, closing my eyes and imagining lifting off the ground like a bird and flying over the trees and rooftops. It was a child's fantasy.

In my early 30's I was camping on Mingus Mountain in the central mountains of Arizona with some friends from work. At the time, I worked at an airline where I earned less than $20,000 per year. I had $36,000 in credit card debt and I paid $200 per month to live in a rental home with two roommates. We took a hike through the forest up a steep grade and, as we came to the crest, we discovered many campers with beautiful multi-colored human sized "kites" set up on a ridge that spanned a sea of air with giant cumulus clouds above. A smooth flow of air streamed up the mountain and caused the streamers attached to trees to flutter. Each pilot queued up in line to launch from a steep ramp opening from the forest to the expanse of sky. One by one each pilot stepped off the ramp into the air and become weightless as his feet left the ground to soar like an eagle. That day at exactly 12:20 PM my dream came into reach.

It was a stretch, but I scraped together $500 to take my first lessons and every Saturday or Sunday for the next 6 months I would set the alarm 6 am to head out to the desert to learn the fundamentals of flying. We would learn how to assemble the rented glider and how to put on the harness and parachute in case of an emergency. We would practice running on flat ground with the wind coming from different directions so we could get comfortable with how the wind interacted with the surface of the glider.

61

We would then practice simple launches and landings from just a few feet up a hill. We did many hundreds of practice runs before incorporating small turns into our routine. It was physically exhausting and minor injuries were common and expected. For many weeks we practiced the fundamentals over and over again.

Then one cloudy Sunday my instructor told me I was ready to fly the mountain – my dream was now a reality. On this day, the landing zone would be five miles away versus the 100 yards away that I was used to. The only difference between what I had been practicing and what I would be doing that day was time and distance. So we drove the landing zone to mentally map out obstacles like power lines and barbed wire fences. We discussed my set-up and approach. To say I was nervous was an understatement! My instructor pointed up at the peak of the mountain so I could see where I would be launching from. We drove an hour to the same launch site where my dream to fly hang-gliders was born.

We set the glider up and did our pre-flight checks. Everything looked good. The wind was light but flyable. It was an overcast day so there wasn't a lot of "lift", but the light breeze as indicated by the fluttering stream told me that I could get off the mountain safely. I stepped up to launch my equipment and waited for conditions to be just right. When I was ready, I yelled the customary command, "clear" and my instructor dropped down to the ground and I ran with everything I had while keeping the glider straight and level. Two steps and the wind picked me up and, for the first time in my life, I felt what it was like to be a bird with the wind in my face. Nirvana.

My flight was short but perfect. I headed directly for the landing zone, did my set up at about 500 feet and as the ground got closer, I lightly pushed the bar forward into a perfect flare and landed on my feet. It was one of the highlights of my entire life. I had stepped out of my comfort zone, invested the time and effort and got to experience something that most humans never will.

I flew all over the country almost every weekend for 7 years and then hung up my wings.

Flying is a mental game and so is business. You must learn the mechanics, but that's the easy part. I have found that the #1 reason why most don't make it is fear … . fear of the unknown … fear of failure … fear of embarrassment and even fear of death. I have also found that by taking on challenges that make me come face to face with my fear, I become better prepared to succeed in business. Over the next 20 years, I applied the mindset skills that I learned flying hang gliders in my Network Marketing business and it allowed me to succeed at levels that most only dream about.

After 20 years I had built a six-figure annual residual income. My Network Marketing business has paid me in excess of $20 million, which has allowed me to achieve many of my lifelong dreams. Some of those dreams include writing two bestselling books, taking at least a one weeklong exotic vacation a month for many years and flying on private jets all over the world. 100% of the profits from my first book, Beach Money have been used to fund loans to entrepreneurs in developing countries through a program called kiva.org that offers micro loans to new business owners that need financing.

One afternoon, I was looking out of the windows from my condo on the Vegas strip watching the helicopters give tours and wondering what it would be like to be a helicopter pilot? What if I could offer rides to my friends and family when they came to town. I wasn't looking for a job flying helicopters. I was considering what it would be like to do this for fun! I needed a new challenge that would stretch me at a level I had never experienced before.

And at the age of 55 years old, I googled "helicopter training in Vegas" and, once again, the adventure began! I achieved the dream of becoming a helicopter pilot at the age of 57 years old and it's one of the most fun and exciting things I have ever done in my life!

There were many times on the journey that I thought about quitting. It was hard and at times quite scary. I had to practice maneuvers and emergency procedures for many hours with an instructor. The day I "solo'd" was a day I will never forget. I was with my instructor Tammy and one day after flying for a few months she said, "You're ready!" I said, "Ready for what?" She said, "You're ready to go on your own." She then told me to land the helicopter. I did and she got out!! She told me to do three "patterns" on my own. It was scary, exciting, fun, exhilarating and massively rewarding. But I had to pay the price!

So here are some of the lessons I have learned from flying that I apply to my Network Marketing business each day:

1. I had to invest $75,000 and about 150 hours to be able to enjoy the dream (just like you must invest in your business: personal development, events, tools and product)

2. I had to make sacrifices (You'll need to make your business a priority and other things will need to take a back seat for a while until you are up and running!)

3. I had to face my fears (I know your fears feel real and the only way to overcome them is to face them head on. The more you practice, the more confident you will become. No way around this.

4. I had to practice the fundamentals (Over and over and over again. In real life ... not just in the classroom. Practicing with real potential customers and distributors will allow you to hone your skills).

5. At one point I had to do it on my own (Soloing ... doing it on your own. It's scary the first few times. But it's the only way to finally get good.)

6. There are things you can't possibly train for so you learn the

fundamentals (When you get served the twists and turns, the fundamentals will get your through).

7. I had to be bad before being good (It's okay to be bad at first. Each time you do it you will get a little better)

8. I had to trust and have faith (trust in my instructors and others have gone before me. Others have gone before you)

9. Living the dream is fun and way better than could possibly be imagined (it's worth it)

MOMENTUM MAKERS
WHY PEOPLE STOP

1. **THEY GET DISTRACTED:** Most people that signed up see their business as just another thing to do. It's on the list, and usually not the highest priority. It keeps getting knocked back because of other "more important" things and eventually just falls off the list.

2. **THEY LOSE EXCITEMENT:** When they signed up, their excitement was at an all-time high. And most people, I think that that excitement will always be there. When they wake up one day, and they are not quite as excited because of a couple of disappointments, they decide it may not be for them. They lose their motivation. They begin to doubt. They question whether it will work for them.

3. **IT WAS HARDER THAN IT SEEMED:** Once they realize that it is going to take some work, and not as many people as they thought would be interested, they begin to question whether it's worth their time. Especially not knowing what the outcome will be. They see how hard others work to achieve a little success and start to wonder whether they have in them to make that kind of a commitment.

DARLA DIGRANDI-AGUILERA
LIVING THE #YESLIFE

I used to be a huge skeptic of Network Marketing. I was the type of person that would tell you "those things don't work" and that "only the people at the top make all the money". You could say writing this now is my redemption opportunity for the damage I caused by being ignorant to something I knew nothing about yet spoke as if I did. I know I successfully encouraged so many people to not take action on what could have led them to their dream life.

When we are born, we come into the world the exact same way. We are like a blank hard drive that gets programmed the second we are born. Our programmers are our parents, those that we are surrounded by, our culture, the school system, and society.

My inspiration to be an Entrepreneur started as a young child. I was very fortunate to experience two completely different lives growing up. On the one hand, I was the child of a single hard-working mother who was very good at what she did. She was a banker to high-profile people. She was paid a salary and worked very long hours. She hated her boss. He was constantly on vacation or golfing and it was her job to cover for him.

Conversely, I was very fortunate to have a good friend whose family I was able to spend a lot of time with. They were very wealthy, and their parents were happily married and always present in their children's lives. They didn't work "traditional" jobs, so they had a lot of time to spend with their family. I was treated as one of the children and saw the value of "present-parenting." With my friend's family, I was able to travel in limousines, they had their own private driver. We ate at expensive restaurants where everyone knew their name. Through them, I became familiar with a completely different type of life. They had a very big house with a 7-day a week cleaning lady, maintenance and service people to take care of them. Popular, political, and high society people were always hanging out there. The conversations in that house were different than the ones in mine. All of that made a huge impact on my life. That was my inspiration for what type of lifestyle I wanted to have.

I knew I was not going to work for a boss, I was going to be the boss and I needed hard working people like my mom, that cleaning lady, the limo driver, the pool man, and those gardeners working for me. This way, I could spend my time doing what I want, when I want, where I want and with who I want. It made total sense to me. I didn't know how I was going to do it I just knew I was going to, and I did. I did it the only way that I knew how at the time. Which was to be a traditional business owner.

I knew it wasn't going to happen the "royalties & inheritance" way – you know, write a song or make a movie and get paid every time it plays, long after you are dead and gone. Then leave that in your will to your unborn grandchildren to carry on your legacy. I wasn't born into that heritage and I couldn't sing or act. Those people are called the 1-5%er's because very few people in the world make that "kind" of money and I don't mean the amount - I mean the means of making money. The kind that pays you over and over again off a one-time effort. The type of money that I knew was not taught in classrooms. If it were, then teachers would be retired and living instead of working their entire life. This is why I appreciate teachers so much!

The only other way I knew to make lots of money was to own high-end salons and spas and have lots of people working for me. So that's what I did. I worked for a boss for a few months, long enough to know that I wanted to be like him; so, I started off on my Entrepreneur journey that eventually landed me in the top 100 Fastest Growing Salons in the country.

However, that wasn't easy! It took me tens of thousands of dollars and endless hours and years of hard work. We had a total of 5 locations and 49 employees, and we serviced 16,000 clients. The bigger our salon enterprise grew, the further away from that dream of traveling the world and being a present-parent was getting. It was clear that path was taking me away from the life I said I wanted when I was younger, but I didn't know how else to get there. I didn't know that there was a different way to make money that would allow me to be free without a lifetime of hard work. Until I found Network Marketing.

Fast forward to a few years ago, at the age of 48 my 80-year-old mother had a conversation with me that made my entire life become crystal clear. It was a talk that launched a fire inside of me to get VERY loud about this industry that is so misunderstood. With tears in her voice on the other end of a phone, she spoke the words that changed my life forever! "Honey, I don't know how you did it but you did. You figured out how to live the life I've always dreamt of having. I wanted nothing more than to be there for your children instead of being at work, but I didn't have anyone like you in my life to teach me how. It was like when your older sister was born. I didn't have a clue what to do with that baby when they put her in my arms. I had never held a baby before in my life and they didn't have classes like they do today to teach you how to care for them".

This industry gave my family the life my mother always wanted. It gave my daughter the childhood I never had. It gave me a marriage my parents never had and allowed me to see a world I never knew I could reach. Now, I'm passionate about making sure as many people as possible know that their dreams can be their reality.

Life is not meant for working, it's meant for living. Being a present-parent is possible and you can raise your own children rather than pay someone else to. You can have a life that allows you to give instead of only receive. The world is full of adventure and, yes, you can afford to see it. The lack of time to be in love is the number one cause for divorce and, yes, you can avoid it. When the majority of time is spent chasing money and the stress of survival, you miss it all.

If you are a skeptic or have a negative taste in your mouth from a past experience, this book is for you. I was that person for many years. I did not believe in this industry AT ALL. Do you remember the blank hard drive we were born with that I spoke about earlier? Mine was full of anti-Network Marketing sentiment.

Today I can say that Network Marketing is the easiest, fastest, and most affordable way I have found in life to reinvent, build, or re-build a "YesLife" rather than a "NoLife." In my salon world of millions, I didn't even realize I had a "NoLife". I was owned by customers and employees. If one of the two didn't show up that day there was no transaction created so there were no profits to be made; yet, salaries and bills still had to be paid. If I were still in the traditional transaction-based business world, I stood no chance of doing many of the things I have done in the past decade of life because, no matter how big I grew in size or how high prices were, it did not come with "time", it only came with "money" and money cannot buy time, it must be intentionally preserved.

It took me 3 years of hard work in the traditional transaction-based world before I made my first penny of profit and that is considered great! We were the biggest and most expensive salon & spa in town. We charged $100 for haircuts, it was nothing for people to drop $300 per visit, we had 49 employees, a total of 5 locations and had a 6-week waiting list and we were debt-free. I say all that to make an impression on you that the bigger we grew the further away we got from a YesLife.

Conversely, in Network Marketing, I invested a few hundred dollars, made my investment back in my first week and made my first million dollars in 3 years and this is how I did it.

When the economy crashed in 2008, it was my blessing in disguise. Had the crash not occurred and rocked the real estate and stock markets, it would not have collapsed our world and created "cause" in my life. My cause was that I needed to make an extra $10k a month to cover my payroll. I didn't know at the time that we were in the beginning stages of losing it all and birthing a new life. Looking back had I of recognized it I would have done it faster. I would have not prolonged the agony by trying to save it all. I was borrowing money from anywhere I could, robbing Peter to pay Paul and spinning plates.

The day it all came crashing down was the day my life began to change. I'll never forget this day in my life. I have played this day over and over millions of times in my mind trying to process the answers of "why didn't I listen sooner" and "why me"? That day was March 26th of 2008. The day the banks pulled back all of the $100,000 credit lines. I was $20,000 overdrawn in my payroll account the day I finally gave in to a local businessman that was driving me crazy for 4 months to take a look at a business opportunity. He said, "I only need 30 minutes" and I told him "Ok, I'll give you 30 minutes but just so you know, I'm not buying anything"!

I believe my skepticism versus faith mind had been testing me. I say that because every night before bed and all day that my eyes were open, I was praying for a way to get out of my situation - looking pretty and strong on the outside and falling apart on the inside. All I wanted was a way to hang on to what I had not lost yet and to not have to lay off the last 25 people. Meanwhile, this local businessman was relentless. Today I am grateful for that man. I personally believe that God was answering my prayers through that man the entire time; but it was me who was blind to see it. It took me getting so far behind and so far into a hole in life to open my eyes to see something in a different way. Today I see that darkest moment in life as my blessing in disguise, very much like the story of "the big flood".

Our daughter is now 16 years old and she has lived a life that most children do not get to. She has traveled for a one-year vacation in a million-dollar RV, she's been to more countries and on luxury vacations than most people do in a lifetime. She has lived both of my lives growing up. She knows how important making certain types of money is and what will take you on the path to a YesLife instead of a NoLife. She knows how to work backwards and look at the big picture of life to see what you want it to be 10 years from now. She knows how to determine how much that life will cost to maintain; and, she knows to examine whether or not it is a life of freedom and travel, or a life chained to working all the time. Will it earn you enough to be a giver or only enough to care for yourself?

When considering a job or a career field. Stop first and think of someone that has been doing that job or career already for 10 years. What is their quality of life like? Does it fit your dream life? If it does, look at HOW it pays, not "how much" it pays. Is it an hourly wage? Is it commission? Is it transaction-based? Does it pay you over and over again off the first transaction? Does it pay you from other people's efforts if you build a network of people? Does it require you to have inventory? What is the overhead? Does it come with a ceiling of what you can make? Does it pay you when you are asleep or only when you are awake and working?

Most people do not know all the ways that money is made. They only know what they were taught in school. The majority of people in the world (95%ers) only know how to work a job and trade their time for money. That is the hardest way on the planet to make a living. However, most people settle in and get stuck there for a lifetime. What started out as a temporary thing became a permanent thing because of the unawareness of what's possible and complacency about what's comfortable.

The ones that do keep moving through the progression of how money is made become self-employed. From there it goes to hiring and training people to work for you which is called "leverage," then onto opening and building which are "units of distribution". Then when profits are made it goes to "investing" into things that pay you a return which then creates "multiple streams of income". If those investments are paying you over and over again, you have "residual-leveraged income" and that is how to capture "time & money" and reach that place of "time-freedom" where you live rather than work.

I have watched hundreds of thousands of people start in Network Marketing only to quit before they made it. They would be living free today had they not quit. The reason they quit is because they didn't realize what they had their hands on. They had the old me in their ear filling them with false information, not the educated me inspiring and encouraging them.

Their blank hard drive was programmed the same way mine was when I was growing up. They were told things like "if it seems too good to be true then run the other way", "nothing comes easy", "go to school, get good grades, so you can get a good job for good pay and retire with stock options, 401k, and benefits", "$100k a year is good money", "only the ones at the top make all the money", "money doesn't grow on trees" and "save your money for a rainy day". Each of these only paralyzes you into living a falsehood that survives as you waste your life chasing a dream you can never quite reach.

Now close your eyes and pretend you are my child and listen to what you would hear today. "if it seems too good to be true, sit down and pay attention because that's where opportunities come from", "making money is easy, working for it is hard", "go to school and get good grades so you can carry on intelligent conversations with others", "the average person thinks $100k a year is good money because they don't believe it can be made in a month so they don't try", "you cannot create wealth with the works of your own two hands, you need an army of hands working for you or with you", "money does grow on trees, let me teach you how to plant the seeds" and "cutting back and downsizing are not ways to get ahead".

Network Marketing cannot only set you free, it can give you a life that you had never dreamt possible. It can allow you the time freedom to find the reason you were born. It will enable you to give yourself a way to make the world a better place. It will allow you to be present in not only your children's lives, but it will also allow you to be there in those "blink of an eye" moments that we don't think of when we are young. Like when our parents get older and need to be cared for or when loved one that takes ill or for a life tragedy that requires our time or when personal illness requires treatment to beat.

Fight the fear and make a change. Find a mentor and get under their wing. Do what they do and be willing to fail until you win. Once you start on your journey inside Network Marketing, do not quit until you win because quitters never win.

MOMENTUM MAKERS

1. **TAKE CONTROL OF YOUR LIFE:** No one can build your life for you. You are the only person who determines how you will spend your minutes on this Earth. If you feel like you are not getting anywhere, it's because that's what you have chosen. From this point forward, choose the path you want to be on.

2. **BUILD YOUR "YESLIFE":** Freedom is everything. It is so easy to become enslaved to things that once meant progress but now holds us back. You will never get to freedom without honestly evaluating the things you are a slave to.

3. **DON'T LET YOUR PAST MURDER YOUR FUTURE:** Past experiences can either give us confidence or fully destroy our confidence. Without taking risks you cannot build a better circumstance than the one you are in. Getting to your dreams requires change and change is a risk. You must be willing to let go of the things telling you, "no."

LAURA WELLS

HEART AND HUSTLE

I almost threw up during my very first home-party due to stage fright… and my party hostess was my mother-in-law. Yeah. I figured it could only get better from there. Thank goodness, it did. And, what I learned from that very first party has stayed with me for nearly 20 years – just be yourself.

I ditched my cue cards, put down my script, and looked out into the living room full of my mother-in-law's bible-study lady friends and said, "I'm super nervous. But I like these products. Can I just help y'all shop and we have a good time? " And so, my career began just like that.

Direct Sales and Network Marketing has held my interest for nearly my entire adult life, and I guess you could say I was destined for it from a young age. I was born and raised in Dallas, Texas. Although I was never personally a Mary Kay consultant, I grew up with Mary Kay's family. Her grandson Ryan and I were close friends from the time we were practically toddlers through elementary school. My mom and dad were good friends with his parents - Richard and Jan Rogers. My mom was an early consultant for Mary Kay and our families always did things together. After my dad passed away when I was 4 years old, our families remained close.

A funny story… my mom, being a single parent in the '80s and '90s, had taught me to never get into ANY car with ANY person unless they had the secret password, even if I knew them. I remember one time when I was in 2nd or 3rd grade, walking home from the bus stop, a stretch limo pulled up next to me and stopped. The back window rolled down, and I heard a man's voice, "Laura, come get in the car and I'll drive you home".

I, being the rule-follower that I was, replied, "What's the secret password?" The man in the limo did not know.

So, I told that man, Richard Rogers (Mary Kay's son) no I absolutely would NOT get into the stretch limo to ride down the street to my house. When I walked in the door a few minutes later, I heard roaring laughter from the living room. The adults thought I was the cutest little thing. I could just imagine all of the "Oh, bless her heart," comments endearingly flying around the very southern living room.

My very early childhood was a pretty lavish life. I didn't know it at the time, as my mom was a hard worker, and very humble. But looking back, there were a lot of experiences including moving to Grand Cayman (that's where I began school, actually), spending the night at friends' gigantic mansions, hanging out at country clubs as kids with an unlimited "tab" for us to put Shirley Temples and sandwiches on, private helicopters for birthday parties, riding horses at a very upscale polo club, and more.

As time passed, life changed. My mom and I moved to Australia for a short time, then to California, then back to Texas. By then, we had lost touch with the Rogers/Ash families. Even though my childhood was surely infused with Mary Kay's family's influence, to a certain extent, I never really knew about direct sales as a profession. Sure, I had heard of Tupperware and Mary Kay as a teenager, but never thought anything of it. My mom worked a lot in my adolescent and teenage years, sometimes even working 2 jobs to make ends meet, and although she was one of the very first Mary Kay consultants for a short time, she was never really involved in direct sales.

In 1992, I met my husband Jeremy (I was 15). I proposed to him when I was 16. He said, "No." I asked him again. He said, "No" again. He proposed to me a few months later. How about that follow up, y'all? He enlisted in the Marine Corps in 1993, and we got married in May of 1994, when I was 17, just after he completed boot camp & combat training.

You probably know enlisted military personnel don't get paid very much. We had our first child, Mason, in 1996 when I was 19 while we were stationed at Camp Pendleton, CA. Even with WIC, and my trust fund, we still had a very hard time making ends meet. My husband served during the escalation of war in the Middle East, and at the time of his re-enlistment, he was given the option to either re-enlist and immediately go to Okinawa, Japan, or exit. He decided not to reenlist. In 1997, he was honorably discharged from the Marine Corps and we set out into Corporate America. He landed a job in Las Vegas where his parents lived at the time, so we moved there.

We had our daughter, Mekenna, in 1999. My husband's career was taking off, and I loved being a stay at home mom. I led a M.O.P. S. chapter at my church for moms of preschoolers, volunteered for the women's ministry at our church, and led a young women's bible study group as a new Christian myself. I love networking with other women and always have - even as a young mom in my early 20s.

When our daughter was around 2, my friend and neighbor invited me to come to a "kitchen show" at her house. It was a direct sales party, and I knew nothing about it. I agreed to go even though I don't like, and definitely was not good at, cooking. I do like eating, and the lady doing the demo would apparently be making a "brownie pizza" and "taco ring" at the party. "Brownies & Pizza?", I'm in! So, I went.

I remember sitting in the hostesses living room, catalog in hand, thinking that it looked like fun doing these types of parties. Everyone was laughing, shopping and, let's not forget, eating… all the things I liked to do. At the end of the party, the consultant had a line of ladies with order forms (and credit cards) in hand. When it was my turn to order with her, I asked her if she would mind sharing how much commission she made from doing these types of parties. When she told me, I thought, "I could totally do that a couple of times a month for some extra 'fun money'".

Maybe for date nights, girl's night out, or the random retail-therapy trip to Target.

So, I came home and excitedly told my husband that I wanted to do this kitchen show thing! He reminded me that I don't like to cook. And that one of my fears was public speaking. "So this gig involves you cooking and speaking at the same time?" I don't remember his exact response to my naive enthusiasm, but it was surely something like "okay, sweetie, I support you". He has always supported my, sometimes questionable, ideas.

In the beginning, Direct Sales was just a hobby that I dabbled in for a few years. It was fun, and when I did the parties, I was good at it. I made some extra money, earned some free kitchenware (that my husband used since he does the cooking usually), and my friends loved having me do the demos for their friends because apparently I was entertaining and helped them shop (hmm, thinking back, I am realizing that most people loved my demos but didn't rave about my cooking results. There was that one time where I did an entire presentation, and at the end, a sweet older lady pointed out that I put sugar in a recipe that called for salt. Okay, whatever! Cooking wasn't my strong suit! I already knew that).

I kind of treated it like a hobby, not really taking it seriously.

Financially, I didn't "need" to make my side-gig work. That is, until 2008 when we had moved from Las Vegas back to the Dallas area after the recession hit and we were impacted by a layoff. Finding a new career during that time was extremely hard and dragged on for months and months - well past the unemployment stipend. Eventually, I found myself standing in the U. S. Welfare office, two kids in tow, filing for funds and food stamps.

All of our savings was depleted.

Our credit cards were maxed.

Stress was high. Jobs were low.

With not many other options, I did what any other rational woman would do... I threw a party. (I know you're like, "What...?")

Using some of the last bit of funds on our "Texas Lone Star" (food stamps) card, I bought food for the party and re-launched my little "home party hobby" to kick things up a notch and make a business out of it for real this time.

Having a single mom like mine that worked tirelessly, without complaint, to give me the best life possible and marrying my husband who led by example with his tenacity and ambition, I learned some things about the importance of having a massive work ethic, thinking outside the box, overcoming, adapting, and doing "whatever it takes".

With the food we purchased with food stamps, my husband made a tray of "Asparagus Roll Ups" and several other appetizers for the re-launch party (including that Taco Ring and Brownie Pizza) and I had one goal: fill the calendar with parties.

From that day forward, I ran. I ran as if our lives depended on it, because truly, at the time, it felt like they did. I wound up at the top of that company in sales & recruiting. I broke several company records, earned multiple awards, trips, stage time, and trophies. Yea, Me!

A few years later, I went to another company, and became one of the top recruiters & top in sales there as well. But I was EXHAUSTED. It was a home-party type business before social media was really a popular thing, I was doing 3-4 parties a week. Although I loved being a stay at home mom (and room mom, field trip chaperone, den leader, girl scout troop leader, etc.) I was not HOME very much because I was out working my "home based" business doing parties.

Through dabbling in online message boards, forums, and the emergence of Facebook, I realized that I could leverage social media to build a business without parties. I loved my home-party hosts in my local area but transitioning to an online business instantly allowed me to reach more people, worldwide. Once I tasted the freedom of truly working from home through Network Marketing, I never looked back.

Fast forward several years, my success in the direct sales industry opened many doors for me to help others. I became the President of a global networking and sales training company for women entrepreneurs, and have been in several advisory roles for executive teams in Network Marketing for social media marketing, compliance, and strategy planning for about 10 years working within the corporate side of direct sales.

Back in the field, I had decided that I wanted to grow a Network Marketing business online without doing parties. Because of that, I have recruited over 1,500 people through Facebook alone (not counting my time doing home-parties in direct sales).

I have seen the guts and behind the scenes. I have seen behind the curtains of Network Marketing, and I love it. Yes, I have experienced crazy things (and crazy people) along the way, but to me, it's like finding your people within any big community. Find your tribe and love them hard. Never settle for less than you deserve.

Just 17 days after joining my current Network Marketing company, we were car bonus qualified. 4 months later, my husband had the option to resign from his full-time career because I was out-earning him, and 1 year later, I was able to resign from my role as president of the company I worked for as well, so we could both be home full time.

Our kids are now adults, and we live in a little town on Lake Chatuge in the Appalachian Mountains of north Georgia. My mom lives in a little cottage on our property. Our house backs up to a large part of the Hiawassee River. It is a "dream home" that we envisioned for many years.

I'm so grateful to each person who has ever said "yes" to my products or business.

I will forever be grateful to Network Marketing. In October 2017, I was diagnosed with a rare cancer (Leiomyosarcoma) and had two surgeries back to back to remove it (praise God, they got it all!). In January 2019, I had a cancer-related scare and wound up with a Hysterectomy. Having two major surgeries in two years meant a lot of time "off work". If it weren't for the freedom for myself AND my husband to both be home full-time... plus the residual income & ability to work anywhere... that would have been *very challenging*. But, aside from recovering physically, it was not a hardship for us.

You never know what's around the corner, my friend.

The best advice I could give you? Dig your well before you're thirsty.

That is what keeps me going. I want to help other people have the comfort of knowing that they've got a cushion when things get bumpy.

Whether you're from Princeton or Prison, the opportunity we have in the Network Marketing profession is equal. The RIGHT kind of work will bring you fun and freedom.

This is an incredible gig for anyone who has an entrepreneurial spirit AND truly has a servant-leadership heart to help others. A lot of people tend to have one or the other, but I believe it's truly important to have both. Heart and hustle.

MOMENTUM MAKERS

1. **BUILD A BUSINESS THAT IS RIGHT FOR YOU**: You need to know your "yes." Getting to it means identifying the things you are really passionate about. Then, build a business around that. Do not create expectations for yourself that you cannot meet. If you do not want to work weekends, do not go into real estate. If you don't like being inside all day, don't get an office job.

2. **DON'T BE AFRAID OF CHANGE:** It is not uncommon to start with one company and then discover that while you LOVE network marketing, the product or company is not the right fit for you. Don't be afraid to switch companies once you get into the business. Many people do. Find the company with the right culture, product and compensation plan for you.

3. **DIAMONDS ARE EVERYWHERE:** You never know which relationships are going to turn into the ones that build your business. Don't write any relationship off. If someone seems interested, give him or her a shot. Remember, someone else took a chance on you.

JAIME PECA

ACCIDENTALLY ON PURPOSE

May 2012 was a very pivotal month for me. I was a young, married mom with two kids under four and drowning in debt. Sound familiar?

My husband and I were juggling our house and our finances. I was attempting to be an A+ mom and be present as a wife for my husband and, on top of that, I was losing who I was with each passing day. Was this what a midlife crisis looked like?

Seven months into maternity leave, with 5 months remaining, I realized we were barely making ends meet; so, I had to go back to work early. My husband and I passed each other as he came home and grabbed the kids and I set out for work. One night, my babysitter invited me to a home party she was having. I was reluctant but knew it would be right around the time I picked the kids up; so, I decided to go. I had developed stretch marks as a mom and it was a product I had wanted to try to help fix them; but financially we just couldn't swing it.

When the party started, my first thought was, "The products are probably some cheap variant on something else and I won't be interested and I'm definitely not starting a business." The host started the party by letting us try the products. I was shocked when I discovered I really liked it and I was already seeing results. While I was surprised that I really wanted the product, I still had a second line of defense. There was no way I was going to start an "illegitimate home-based business.",

And then, it began…the hostess unveiled the business pitch.

My eyes rolled as she presented the compensation plan. In my head I thought, "Oh Lord, here comes the pyramid scheme." Luckily, my son began to get fussy; so, I used the excuse that I couldn't stay because I had to get him home. However, I knew I wanted to try the product and my sitter had joined that evening to become a rep. So, I grabbed a computer as fast as I could, signed myself up through her link and got myself out of there before I got reeled into selling something, which I swore I would not do.

On my way home I called my friend, also a new mom, to tell her about the awesome results I was already having. I was so thrilled that something actually worked on me and I couldn't wait to get the products in my hand. My girlfriend had the same issues, so she asked me for the link to buy. I gave her the link to my babysitter's new distributor account, and she signed up on the spot. I showed a few more of my close friends the results I had from the products and OMG everyone was blown away and asking for the link.

When I got to my computer, I saw the email confirmation for my order; I couldn't wait to get my hands on the products! The only problem was, it thanked me for my order AND welcomed me to the team as a distributor!?! Umm, PARDON?? What did that mean?

At that moment I realized that in my panic to get out of the party, I must have ordered as a distributor instead of simply becoming a customer. My heart sank and I felt a bit sick. All I could think was, "I don't want to sell this!" What would my friends think? What would my family think? OMG, "I'm that crazy lady from down the road who people will run from if they know I'm in Network Marketing." But then the light bulb went on. I'm pretty sure NONE of those people pay my mortgage or my grocery bills so why did I care? My real friends should support me and cheer me on. Maybe I COULD do this! After all, I was already doing it by giving my friends my babysitter's link. I just wasn't getting the benefit. Maybe this was a blessing in disguise standing right in front of me and this could be the vehicle that changes my family's future…and boy was I right.

With butterflies in my stomach, I decided rather than canceling that distributor account, I was going to see if I could take a bit of the financial stress off our family, regardless of whether or not the people around me judged me or, worse, blocked and deleted me off social media. I worked harder than I think I ever worked in my life with my first company. I joined by accident but stayed because I saw a way to earn a $10,000 bonus that we so desperately needed.

I talked to everyone, I became vulnerable and showed the before and after pictures of my lovely stretch marks I earned as a new mom. What helped me explode though was showing all the people who joined me how to see success and we locked arms and ran together. In the 5 years I was with that company, I had success but major failures as well. I had rock stars join my team and then fizzle out; I dragged people along who said they wanted to run with me and do the work; but, eventually, they must have disappeared into the witness protection program because I never heard from them again. I convinced a lot of people to order or to join, which led to frustration and exhaustion because they were not the right people. I never gave up and I always moved forward; but I felt like I was losing my fire for Network Marketing.

I am an entrepreneur at heart, so I started my own business at home and let my first shot at Network Marketing fizzle out. With the new venture, I was tired and exhausted, and I missed the community aspect of Network Marketing so much!

I found another company that I had been seeing for months and needed to try the products. I seriously fell in love with what they sold but was so scared to jump back into Network Marketing. I had worked so hard at all the wrong things and did not want to go through that again… I knew if I was ever to do it again there would be a few key things I would look for.

1. A Proprietary Product: A company with a patented "sizzle" product. Something no one else had and everyone would want to try.

2. A Debt Free Company: This was so important to me because I didn't want to jump in and bust my booty for a company that could close its doors tomorrow and leave me with nothing.

3. A Company That Invests Well: A company that is smart with their money and invests it in the right places will not only last but build a great foundation for my future. It's great to be debt free but if they are out buying islands and massive buildings instead of putting it back into R&D and staying innovative and giving it back to customers and promoters in the field then how will they stay on top and remain relevant?

4. An Early Stage Company: A company that is early in its lifecycle that has a fresh product and perspective is one in which my level could grow with it.

5. A Company with Strong Character: A company with integrity and vision! I needed to trust and love the CEOs and corporate staff who run and make decisions for the company. I don't always have to agree with where they go but I need to know that their decisions are always in the best interest of the company and the people building it, rather than them.

6. A Great Compensation Plan: I needed to love the compensation plan and really understand all the ways we get paid. It had to be duplicable and something I could show a brand-new person how to see money in the first few weeks of them starting. After all, asking people to wait for weeks to see any mullah or even worse over a month and in the meantime ask them to pay for autoshipments and websites before they saw any money just didn't sit right with me.

So how did I find massive success in the world of Network Marketing… follow along. I'll share with you how I joined a company and hit the TOP rank in 42 days, became the number one earner in Canada and in 17 short months became a Millionaire with that company.

I am a big believer that ignorance on fire is better than knowledge on ice. I know, I know, you are probably asking yourself "What does that even mean?"

"Ignorance on Fire" means you don't need to know everything to get started. You just need to be passionate and run with the excitement you have. Just start!! Too much information can paralyze people and bog them down with details that are unnecessary. Set a goal, decide that you won't let your excuses get in the way of success and that you will go all in with your business even when things get tough.

The success I had in my company had nothing to do with how much I knew about the compensation plan, or all the ingredients in my products. My success was built on my excitement and passion and I wanted to share what I had my hands on with everyone! I was laser-focused on what I wanted to achieve and right out of the gate I decided my non-negotiables for both my family and myself. I sat down with my husband and kids and we talked about what the next 45 days was going to look like. I knew I was going to miss some kids' activities and that my husband was going to have to pull double duty and take over things I usually took care of. I told them I needed their support more than ever. I pulled out a calendar and scheduled as many calls as I could. I showered less than I would like to admit and ate most meals right from my bed. I slept only a few hours a night and was right back at it even on days I didn't want to or that fire was dimming, or my mommy guilt was kicking in for missing my kids' events or time with my husband. I CHOSE (yes this is an absolute CHOICE) to not let my WHY for doing this, my family, also become my excuse for why I couldn't.

I couldn't in one breath say I was doing this for my family and in the next breath not show up for my business because of my family time. It was an investment I was making, on an opportunity that most take for granted. I knew that if I gave it a thousand percent that I could change my family's lives and show everyone that with a lot of hard work and dedication I could and would do this.

Network Marketing is the way of the future. Too many people are struggling to pay for housing and groceries and running out of money before the end of the month. A lot of people can't afford the time and the fuel it takes to be at a regular JOB each day. Find a company that excites you and run!! Make a plan and give it 3-5 years of hard hustle. It won't happen overnight and it may take longer for you than someone else. Stay laser-focused and don't give up. Plug in and stay connected to leaders who inspire and push you.

So, TODAY make a decision that can change your life if you let it.

Take it ONE day at a time; Rome wasn't built in a day. Don't compare yourself to others. Comparison is the thief of joy. It doesn't matter what others are doing. All that matters is what YOU are doing.

Surround yourself with positivity and people who push you to be greater.

Visualize your goals and then create a vision board. Have them somewhere where you can see them and check them off.

Be kind to yourself and recognize progress no matter how small it is. If you are moving forward, then you are headed in the right direction.

Ask for help when you need and surround yourself with hard working inspirational people in your profession.

In order to be the top 1% in this industry, you have to do what the other 99% won't do!!

You, my friend, are reading this book for a reason. You have got what it takes and will do great things if you put a plan together, decide that your BS excuses are non-existent and that you will push when it gets tough!

You are power and are about to move mountains!

MOMENTUM MAKERS

1. **STRATEGY IS PLANNING FOR TOMORROW TODAY.** "Planning" is the working word. You can dream about tomorrow for the rest of your life and you'll likely never get there. You must take the time to plot your course to your dream and then execute the plan.

2. **COME TO PLAY BALL:** Getting ahead means overcoming. There will likely be thousands of people in your company. If you're shooting for the top, you must be willing to outpace the rest of the people in your company. Your hard work will be contagious.

3. **BE THE FORCE THAT DRIVES OTHERS TO SUCCEED:** It doesn't matter what you know. Your company has likely been around a long time and has a proven track record of success. You don't need to reinvent the process. Trust the process. Just start moving. When you do, people will be motivated by your momentum and everyone will win together.

PETER & SUSIE BAGWELL

PEOPLE MATTER

"Who are you?" That question can often be intimidating for a number of reasons. Depending on the audience, you may find yourself guarded and have a tendency to introduce yourself only based on aspects of your life that you think will be important to the person you're getting to know; for example, it is not uncommon for people to introduce themselves by saying what they do. On other occasions, you might find yourself letting it all out and revealing your innermost dreams and aspirations, even if you haven't really attained all of those goals yet. However, the most important answer to that question isn't what you tell other people, but what you tell yourself.

As we look back on the important milestones in our businesses, we've come to realize that figuring out why we do the things we do is very closely connected to who we are and who we want to be. I remember Jordan Adler explaining in his book *Beach Money* how much of his success was based on the connections he had made with people before he became more financially successful. This foundation of making connections with people seemed to have been more than just a business technique; it became part of who he is, and why we believe he became successful.

An important feature of success is that it often requires the investment of others, those who will buy your products or services or who will invest other resources of time and energy to help you reach your goals. Are you the type of person who is concerned about the well-being of all those people? Do you believe that the way you use your time and energy and resources will benefit them in the long run? Are you willing to make sacrifices to help them now or in the future? Identifying who you are in this regard, and who you want to be, can help you reach those innermost dreams and aspirations.

Even more significant is the answer to the next question: "Does the thought of engaging in those activities make you happy?" All of us desire to be happy. Although the struggles and trials of life weigh us down, sometimes to an unbearable degree, the light at the end of the tunnel is often dependent on the combined efforts of many people. Finding a way to be happy while connecting with these other people has been our key to success.

A significant memory was created for us while we were running our day spa. Peter was still working in his engineering career but worked at the spa's front desk on the weekends. Susie had just brought out a client and taken the next client into the treatment room. After the customer had paid, Peter stared in disbelief as she walked out of the building. He remembered something about her.

"Excuse me ma'am," he exclaimed. "Didn't you come in with a cane?" He remembered when she arrived earlier that morning she was walking with a cane. When the two made eye contact, their happiness about the moment became hard to contain. The client was extremely happy that the treatment had brought her significant relief. Peter felt a strong sense of happiness deep inside realizing that the work they were doing was about much more than just earning income.

But where did the connection start? It had started years earlier when Susie's desire to help others set in motion a business plan that would lead to opening the day spa. Additionally, it was something Peter and Susie decided to do together as a couple. Although they eventually closed the spa to be free from the constraints of running a brick and mortar business so they could help people on a much grander scale, the connection was made because of who Susie was and became a significant part of their foundation for future growth.

Connections with people in our day-to-day life are the foundations of all our activity. Those connections will influence our habits, our speech, our work, and our dreams. Often when contemplating why we do what we do, we discover deep-seated motives and desires, some of which have roots we can't even remember from long ago in our childhood. This requires letting down the guards, the kinds of guards we feel when someone asks who we are.

Some of these motives are selfish, and that's ok, we all deserve to be happy. But when we are asking ourselves who we are we must accept the reality that the combined effect of everything we do affects others more than it affects us. We might decide to do something to make ourselves happy, but when we do something to make others happy, we also lay a long-term foundation for ourselves. This foundation is a networking opportunity.

If we could give you a few hundred of our friends, how would that work? Let's say we were going on a trip and handed you our little black book with a couple hundred contacts. Could you just call a few up and make dinner plans? Could you reach out to them in the morning to schedule a brainstorming session in the afternoon? Would any of them be available to you for a round of golf?

Likely, none of the aforementioned contacts would get you very far. Although we have some very generous and happy friends, the truth is that the foundation of those relationships was based on happy connections we made with them over many weeks, months, and years of our life. They are actually the foundation of who we are. You've probably heard the saying "show me your friends and I'll show you who you are".

Although this is a very true statement, it is not the end of your story, but really the starting line of your networking opportunity. At this point in time, you have an incredible opportunity to start making happy connections in every area of your life where you interact with people. Each interaction is an opportunity. Unfortunately, when many people are presented with the idea that each interaction is an opportunity, they react by fire-hosing everyone they meet from the unsuspecting waitress to their long-lost cousin with a sign-up form and price guide.

The solution to happy connections goes back to deciding on the course that will bring those we meet the greatest amount of happiness. Is your business opportunity going to be the connection in your relationship and be the thing that brings them the greatest amount of happiness? If you meet someone new and are currently just trying to get out of the rain, would not the best thing you could do for them be to hold the door open, or assist them with their umbrella?

Your business opportunity isn't likely the key that opens the door to building a relationship. In fact, it may never be. But once the door is open, now you have the opportunity! If you can become the type of person who is concerned about the wellbeing of others, if you believe that the way you use your time and energy and resources will benefit them in the long run, then your natural interest in them will improve the connection.

We have seen and experienced the effect that people, who are constantly at work making others happy, unwittingly and sometimes unknowingly are able to create the most productive networks. This belief isn't a blind faith that comes from hearing an influential person describe some future success or dream. It's also not just a 'what goes around comes around' philosophy. It's a reality rooted in the foundations of connections made helping others – in other words, it's been our real experience.

The deeper the foundation, the stronger the connection is. One of our top team members was enrolled through a phone call with little to no information about the business. She happened to be driving across the country, and we explained that when we found this opportunity, she was one of the first people we thought of. We knew she would enjoy it, we wanted to do it with her, and we truly believed it was a perfect match for her situation. How could she join with such little information? She knew based on previous interactions that we were looking out for her best interests.

So how can we make these deep connections with so many people? After all, there are only so many hours in the day! Just as writing letters and talking on the phone were staples of good communication only a few decades ago, social media has changed the way much of the world communicates. Embracing **a** social media platform or app, not **all** of them, can help you build new foundations in your network.

Social media, local events of nearly any kind, various forms of recreation and even shopping can provide opportunities to learn about people and find out what you can do to make them happy. Did you learn online that someone you know just had a surgery? Did someone you met locally need help figuring out where to buy some product or service? Did someone you meet while exercising need help figuring out a schedule so they can continue to participate? Building blocks in these relationships may be as simple as making a kind phone call to show you care, share information about a deal you found, or let them know how you dealt with a similar challenge they are facing.

Is it that easy? Yes, but to make those connections you need the phone number. In order to get the phone number, you need to be a friendly person who is somewhat willing to engage people selflessly. And to meet that person, you need to be out there, either online or in person to start the connection.

Sometimes we meet someone, and in getting the conversation going we begin to share our story. However, it's not unusual anymore for people to interrupt us and explain that they already know many of the details about our story or our company from what they have already read online or in social media. They came to the event to meet us in person and are often interested in joining our team before they even meet us.

Regardless of how the connection is started, people will join your team when they believe it is going to make *them* happy. Who are you? Have they learned that you are the type of person who is concerned about *their* well-being? Do they truly believe that the way you use your time and energy and resources will benefit *them* in the long run?

We hope you have learned that identifying who you are in this regard, and building connections based on mutual happiness leads to the investment from others that is required to make you successful.

MOMENTUM MAKERS

1. **YOU ARE RECRUITING YOUR INVESTORS:** Often we are so anxious to talk about what we're doing that we forget that our job is to win others over. Whether someone is investing their money or their contacts or their knowledge, they are investing. Make their investment in you valuable to them.

2. **PEOPLE FIRST, PRODUCT SECOND:** Your product will rarely establish your relationships. If you lead first with your product, your relationship will only last as long as their interest in your product. You want people to get to know you first. The product will take care of itself over time.

3. **BE DRIVEN BY THE GOOD, NOT THE MONEY:** You have an opportunity to change people's lives. If you only care about making money, people will know, and you will miss out on the greatest gift of all. Money will follow your success at investing in others and generosity.

KELLY BRYANT

WHEN THE CHIPS ARE DOWN, YOU HAVE A CHOICE TO MAKE

I was a struggling single mom, who felt a little lost in life, but really, my true journey started, "Way back when."

I spent my 20s and 30s wishing, hoping, dreaming about being a mother! As the years passed, I began to think I wasn't going to get the joy of being a mom! I didn't give up hope because I knew, like I knew, like I knew some little tiny being deserved the love I had to give! And, yes, one day I became a mom when I least expected it...IN MY 40's! Being a mom was my greatest joy!! Even though I was so excited, I was also a little scared because I was going to be doing this alone, not by choice, but by circumstance!

When my son was born, I had been a business professional for 20+ years working 70 plus hours a week! I was a workaholic by necessity.

And like most Americans, I was not living the dream! I was slaving away, living paycheck to paycheck, without savings, nor retirement, and my car was on its last leg...my life was really falling apart. Of course, it wasn't anything I voiced to people and no one would have looked at me and thought I needed an opportunity to drop in my lap.

So off I went, doing the best I could to raise this boy child that I was so blessed to have in my life. As the years went by one by one, it was becoming clear to me that being a single mother required compromise on the one thing I never thought I'd compromise; spending time with my son.

I remember having a fleeting thought when he was 4 years old that I was going to need to be "supposedly" retiring at the same time he would need to be going to college and I didn't know what in the world I was going to do because I didn't have the money for either.

But you do what all good parents do, you just keep going and doing what you do to provide for yourself and your child! The rat race continued!

Unfortunately, my son was always the first one in the daycare and the last one being picked up and it broke my heart because this wasn't the life I wanted my son to have. God gave me this child and I just knew that I couldn't do this to him. I'd longed for a child all my life and I felt like I was failing him as his mother.

When I look back over the few years before I started pursuing Network Marketing, that one moment in time when I had the realization of my needing to retire and my son's need to go to college was one of the most defining moments in my life. I believe it was what allowed me to be open to Network Marketing. I was DESPERATE for a different life.

So my journey began like many others! My really amazing and longtime friend introduced me to a product that instantly changed my life! She said she was thinking about selling it and I loved it so much, I said, "Me Too." And that moment was my first introduction to Network Marketing! So I'd like to believe that I didn't find Network Marketing; it found me.

I took a huge leap of faith and stepped in. Over the next year, I began to share the product and the opportunity, and I built a small team of people. I gained incredible insight into exactly how to become a leader! But in the end, this place wouldn't turn out to be my home.

Because of the vast experience I gained over that year, I was able to recognize where my new home was going to be and because Network Marketing is also about relationships, I developed a close friendship with someone, and she came to me and said, Get $500 and meet me at my place tomorrow! "Wait? What?" I was still working 70 hours a week, still a single mom, still building a team with my present company and I didn't know how I would find another second in the day!

But I think life brought me here to this exact moment!

And when my friend shared the details of the most incredible and unique opportunity: we were first in the marketplace, we had a very unique product and the comp plan was out of this world and if you were able to get yourself to a rank that was midlevel in the comp plan, you would get into a revenue sharing pool and share 1 percent of the revenue of the company and it paid you cash every quarter on top of your residual income and the company was going to be launching in four days.

So at that moment, I knew I had to say yes! I said yes even though we didn't have the products to try. I was willing to risk paying the money to join, knowing that if I lost the money because the company didn't work, I just lost it.

But I knew my work ethic and I knew it was going to be work and I didn't care! It was really the first time I had true deep down hope in a better future.

So I hit the ground running with a burning desire. You might ask yourself, how is it even possible to do more? It is possible because I knew if I could get where I wanted in the company, I would be able to see the light at the end of the tunnel. I could see that my life was going to be different. I could see that retirement was within my grasp. I could see a college fund was so close I could taste it and that FUELED me and I WAS going to make this happen. I was able to fit this business in the nooks and crannies of my life because I believe in the outcome.

Along the way in my journey, I heard someone say, "Don't Let Your Kids Be The Reason Why You Don't Do This, Let Them Be The Reason You Do!" That resonated with me. On the days it got hard because I was having to take my son with me to meetings and events and he cried because he didn't want to go, I would remind myself of that saying – I'm doing this for him. It became my mantra. I knew that it was my job to fight for our future and this beautiful opportunity had dropped in my lap and I was not going to let it pass me by!

The first year came and went and I managed to hit the rank that allowed me to get in the revenue sharing pool. It took sharing my product and opportunity with tons of people. It took learning not to be affected by those that said no. It took consistency. It took learning to be a leader and leading by example! It wasn't easy, but I wouldn't trade it for the world!

But what I learned after that first year was even more valuable. The funny thing about Network Marketing is after you go through your warm market, the people you know, you have to then learn even more skills – how do I get people I don't know excited about this!

They say Network Marketing is personal development with a paycheck. Meaning, the more you delve into personal development and put the principles into play in your life and business, the bigger your paycheck gets. I've found that to be absolutely true! Little did I know that personal development would become a passion of mine.

One thing I know to be true is, I never went to my J. O. B. over those 20+ years wishing to be a better person every single day. HA! I beat the system. I guess the truth is, I was too busy and overwhelmed to even consider it.

This industry and my company, in particular, teach about gratitude! They lead by example in the most phenomenal ways. It's an inspiration and I am following in those footsteps and finding more ways to give.

I've now been with this company I call home for 5 years and growing! After the first couple of years in the business, I became a 6-figure-a-month income earner and was able to semi-retire from my profession. I have the luxury of freelancing in that field when and if I want to. I get to be a stay at home mom with my little boy, who is now 11 years old. I was so blessed to have won a Cadillac SUV in a drawing my company did at their first convention. It happened on stage in front of 900 people. And the company graciously paid the sales tax – I will be forever grateful.

The summer came and I took my son and we drove 10,000 miles across the US. It was the first summer I had off and was able to spend this incredible quality time with him. Best summer ever!!

When I look back at the blessing that Network Marketing has been to my life, I am in complete awe! When I was guided to say yes all those years ago, God knew what was ahead of me! Little did I know how desperately I was going to need to have time to spend with my son! Last year, my son got diagnosed with a very rare muscular dystrophy that affects his heart and most people by the age of 20 need a pacemaker. Wow. Wow. Wow. It was a shocker to my system! I cried for weeks! I cried for his future that I dreamed of for him.

Because of Network Marketing, I wasn't forced to go to a job and sit there and mourn the life I thought we were going to have! I got to do it quietly in my home and heal on my own time while I still received residual income.

But most importantly, this Network Marketing business I have has allowed me to be able to be home with my son and I did heal because I decided to really live even more. I am making the choice to make memories! I haven't told my son the extent of his issues because I wanted him to just be a little boy! I didn't want him to live scared and we will face things together as they come.

When I count the blessings of what Network Marketing has provided in my life, I could never forget to mention the most amazing people that have shown up who became friends in the beginning but now feel like family! I get to travel the world with them, some trips the company pays for and some trips we take on our own to continue to build our business.

I have been blessed by God's awesome grace that Network Marketing found me and I was open to it. This business and this industry have meant the world to me! I wouldn't be WHERE I am without it. I wouldn't be WHO I am without it. For that, I will be eternally grateful for this industry!

MOMENTUM MAKERS

1. **ONE SMALL RISK CAN BUILD A LIFETIME:** Growth always requires change. Hope alone never produces anything. You must take a step towards what you want. It can be scary and it can end poorly; but, without taking that step, you'll never get to your dreams.

2. **GRATITUDE IS THE GIFT THAT KEEPS ON GIVING:** There is nothing you will accomplish without the help of others. It is so easy for us to get focused on our progress and not pay attention to the efforts of others who help us get to it – sometimes their decisions are small but their impact is massive and sometimes it's the opposite. Regardless of the size of their effort or the result of it, you need all of them to get where you want to go.

3. **NEED CAN BE THE GREATEST MOTIVATOR:** When the chips get down, you have a choice to make. You can either give up or go after what you want. The zebra always runs the fastest when the lion is on its backside. Don't let your ebbs in life take hold of you. Turn them into a great reason to get focused and go after it.

RESIDUALS ROCK

What do you know is in your blood? What did you dream of doing as a child? Did you fly away as a pilot? Save the day as a police officer? Entertain the masses as a Hollywood actor? Maybe you dreamt of holding a Nobel Peace Prize. How did you decide the path to travel? Something magical happens when you feel it in your very being. Since both of my parents were entrepreneurs, I had the entrepreneur spirit in my blood.

Growing up I watched both parents succeed on their own path. My dad owned a very lucrative custom home company. When I was young, my mom was a beautician, and as I grew older, she became a licensed massage therapist and reflexologist, who owned her own company.

I tried the corporate environment for 9 years. I sat behind a desk as an accountant for Home Depot. I became desperately tired of sitting behind a desk and not being home with my family. In 1993, I was pregnant with our second child and I knew with all of my heart, this time I didn't want to miss all the "firsts" with him like I did with our first child because I was working all the time. At the same time, quitting it all to sit home, eat Bonbons and watch soaps all day was not an option or even a desire.

As a wife, I knew I needed to and wanted to help my husband support our family. If we both "worked," he didn't have to work several jobs and we both could be a part of our children's lives. Brilliantly, I found things I could do from home. After a quick discussion, we got our first credit card. The Internet had arrived, and this brand spanking new piece of plastic was going to allow me the opportunity to get a shiny giant-sized computer. My parents' ideals for life and passion for entrepreneurship had finally boiled to the top. I could see stars in my future as I started BMD Enterprises, which is my web/graphics, branding and marketing company.

It is amazing how a leap and a desire led me to designing and creating websites for clients all over the world. One very special client changed my life, even more! That very special client was my mom, who introduced me to Network Marketing. Although, at that time, I didn't know what that term even meant, but boy, did I learn the name actually says it all. ;) A health machine is what she sold. Yes, she was with a company that sold a health machine. It was a one-time sale, but if people bought it, you got a commission and if others became reps, and sold it to others you got a percent of what they sold.

A perfect concept. Making money when you aren't even working. I thought it was the coolest thing! Creating my mother's webpage so she had a central hub to sell this crazy $500 health machine gave me a view into how successful she was. I was extremely surprised by how many people purchased this $500 machine without knowing much about it other than what they saw on our website. My surprise and curiosity had me. I decided to get a piece of this Network Marketing pie, so I signed up under my Mom. My mom was seeing benefits from my curiosity and getting her piece of my work. Now I could also profit from the sales of the site I lovingly created. I didn't know anything about the machine other than what Mom told me to put on the site. The compensation plan wasn't something I knew much about, but I sure did enjoy cashing the checks!

Being a people lover, I created an email list to keep in touch with the people who bought as a customer, as well as one for people who bought and became a reseller. Creatively using that not so shiny computer, I also designed thank you cards on my computer, printed them out and mailed to everyone. Keeping in touch grows relationships. I decided I could simply add my new friends to my Christmas card list and add quick check-ins or touches throughout the year. This wasn't the only way we added benefit to who we were as entrepreneurs. People always want to know what is in it for them. How could we make them important? A gigantic light bulb turned on.

Listening to people. When we listen to a person, we instantly make them feel important. We established a conference call line. Once a month I would run a call, and people could call and ask my Mom health related questions and she would answer. We did all these things to build the relationship with all of our clients and customers, as well as our team, and also people who were interested but did not initially purchase. Entrepreneurs have to make a name for themselves — a way to stand out — a brand. Successful entrepreneurs always have a brand related to the benefits they provide and the relationships they create.

Every decision is a section of our path leading us deeper into our passion and our purpose. Joining my mom in the health machine sales industry led both of us to a few different companies, and a new section of the path was paved. The foundation was there. Can you believe a health machine allowed me to realize how good I was at establishing websites, connecting with people, and finding ways to keep in touch consistently to build the relationships, which led people to openly and freely (without me asking) refer me to others? It happened. It happened because I was freely open to a path, sought a passion and a purpose, and bridged people together.

I was hooked. Whatever my parents had, it was officially part of my life forever. Now, I wanted to do better than what I was doing and how I was doing it. This decision led to my personal development journey. Above and beyond simply reading about personal development, I was taking the necessary actions to live it. Reading sales books, I explored and learned all these processes I was currently doing were things "the top" sales trainers taught! Let's give some credit where credit is due. When I was 5 years old, my wise grandmother taught me if someone gives you something or does something for you, you need to thank them properly for it, as they didn't have to do it. Gratitude was learned and secured in my heart at a very tender age.

Needing to share this appreciation for life and people, I continued to join a few network-marketing companies, mostly in the health field because of my Mom. Although I had been a part of a few of these companies, to that point, I had still never heard the term "Network Marketing." I understood the term "reseller." The process was simple. If I became a reseller, bought product, and if others bought as well, I got a percentage off from what they bought and what others whom they referred bought. My understanding went even further because most people stop there. When I kept that up and kept in touch with them and continued to let them know about new products or reminders, they usually bought more. And, more than just buying, it enhanced how much they bought and how many people they referred.

In every company I joined, I made several thousand dollars a month. I was making thousands a month by working from home, doing everything online, and through emails and faxes. Wow! Just saying the word "fax," that is dating it! I was making thousands a month without the glorious help of social media. Yes, people were actually successful before Facebook, Twitter, Instagram, and YouTube. Despite not having social media, we did have something called yahoo groups to keep in touch with clients and customers.

Without any training 2002 came along and I found myself in one magnificent place — making five figures a month. It was just my mom and me. We didn't know who our up-line was or even if we even had one, as they never reached out to us. You would think with our success they would have desired to know what in the world we were doing. No matter the lack of communication from "above in the company," I always kept in touch with everyone my Mom or I brought into the companies.

Why is keeping touch, reaching out to connect, sharing our lives so important? I could move to China or Egypt, start another adventure, and still have people who liked me, trusted me, and knew I would offer them an opportunity they should be a part of with me. Consistently and constantly adding to my family and friends list. Boy, when friends and family plans existed in the cell phone companies — they would have despised my list! I could have talked to the world for free!

You can imagine how much time I was investing in designing, creating, and sending cards. You can see the endless lists of people and their contact information. Spending money on printing and cards and stamps. Time to address all those envelopes. What if something happened to my computer? Now, of course, that dusty, out-of-date computer, which had been purchased by that first piece of plastic had been upgraded several, several times. But, even with the best technology at my fingertips, what would happen if a glass of water was spilled. What would happen to my list and my creations? All that time spent?

At the beginning of 2004, my path took a fascinating new step in my life journey. This step led me to another company, which automatically printed all the cards I sent out to keep in touch with clients and customers. I didn't have to do my own printing, thus saving time and ink. My printer could last longer. No more running to the store for ink in the middle of night. Hand cramps from addressing envelopes would be an activity of the past. And, stamps — who needs them? Plus, if I decided to go swimming with my computer, I didn't have to worry about losing my years of meeting new people and forming new connections. This company would house all of their information. And, back it up too!

To make it more unbelievable, I found out I could be a reseller with them as well. And, I just knew all my clients needed to be using this magical service to keep in touch with their clients. It all made sense. My purpose and passion had truly been connected. I loved making the connections and with this find, and I had the opportunity to help others love making and keeping the connections too! Connecting with ease. Connecting with confidence. As I understand connecting is not everyone's cup of sweet tea, I believe in sending a person out into the business world and thing we call life with knowledge, wisdom, and a card that says, "I am there for you." I can do this because I knew my mom was there for me. My grandmother shared wisdom before I even knew it was wisdom and how I would apply it. Once we have information, once we understand our purpose, once we desire to achieve our passion, it is then we should be sent out into the world to change it. Connecting changes everything. Your business, your life, the world.

Now, for over 15 years, I have been with that marvelous company. It is one of the best tools in my toolbox that I recommend to anyone in business. I freely refer as others refer me or send referrals to me. It is gratitude. It is the law of reciprocation.

Of course, you can't, well shouldn't, put all your business tools in one basket. With the establishment of social media, I also have groups for customers, affiliates/resellers, prospects, so I can keep in touch that way on Facebook. When it comes to sending out news or information, I also have an email list. Zoom is a perfect tool to utilize for team trainings, meetings with prospects, 3-way calls with referral partners and their prospects and/or teams.

Over the course of my time here on earth and in the business world, one of the biggest things I have learned is the fact and value of keeping in touch. Like I said, when I was chartering my way in my inauguration companies, while I never heard or knew the term "Network Marketing" or "Multi-Level Marketing," I just simply knew if I bought and referred others, I made money. And, I knew and understood, if and when they referred others, I could and would earn even more.

As each step built something new and fabulous, as each tier of income arrived, I also learned the more I kept in touch through different avenues such as texting, phone calls, video calls, in person like coffees, lunches, dinners, emails, social media, and tangible touch through the mail, I was building the right kind of relationships with people. I was constructing the avenue that got them to know me, then into the like me, and then to trust me because of who I was in the world, my actions matching my words and by providing extra benefits. That avenue wears a gold sign because it also allows people (clients, customers, potential clients and customers, friends, and even times — family) — to remember me. When they are thinking about some who does anything thing from the list of things I do — websites, marketing, speaking, training, coaching, the now added vocabulary word — Network Marketing — they think of me. If I can, you too can increase sales and referrals.

We are all granted tools every day. Tools come in ideas. They come in wisdom. They come in dusty, dirty, old humongous computers. They come in opportunities. They come when someone says, "Hello, how are you doing today? I just wanted to check in and say, 'You are amazing!'" What tools have you passed up? What tools are right in front of your face? I have to ask, as it is truly part of who I am.

Who would have imagined when I was a young mom, desiring to stay closer to home to see her son take his first steps that I would become financially independent? Who would have imagined that Home Depot Accountant would own several businesses and follow in the footsteps of her entrepreneur loving parents? Who would have imagined that a mom who just wanted to help with the bills would have found a tool that makes relationships run effectively, efficiently, and brilliantly. Who would have imagined that girl who started off by helping her mom would organize groups that help countless across social media deal with the darkness of life?

I am a mother of four. I am a business owner of five companies and three non-profits. I am a traveler. I am a branding and social media coach. I am a speaker. I am a connector. I am ready to connect. Laurie Delk may be my name, but I am known so much more by my connections, personally and professionally due to the relationship marketing that I implement.

MOMENTUM MAKERS

1. **EVERYONE HAS SOMETHING TO SAY:** Have you ever been in a conversation when you feel like a waterfall of words is pouring down on your head? Have you sat waiting and waiting for a space of air in the conversation so that you could just get "one word in edgewise?" What would change about your conversations if you entered each one believing that's how the other person feels? Would you approach it differently? Listening builds relationships. Talking builds a wall of words that can feel impenetrable. Practice the art of letting others go first.

2. **KEEP IN TOUCH:** When you're building a business, your life can easily become consumed with what you're trying to accomplish. If someone you meet does not meet your need, you may pass over them so you can focus on the relationships that build your business. You never know when someone's "no" may change to a "yes." Keep your relationships sincere. Some people may say "no" and simply watch you over time to see how it goes and then become one of your most profitable relationships.

3. **OPPORTUNITIES RARELY COME WITH NICE BOWS:** You have to discover how to use the opportunities that come to you. Never stop asking the question, "How can I turn this chance into a life changing event?" Keep your eyes and heart open. Your whole life could change tomorrow – don't miss it.

CHRISTY FECHSER

THE NOT SO PERFECT BEHIND-THE-SCENES LOOK AT SUCCESS

My first ever encounter with a Network Marketing company was over 20 years ago. I had just moved to a new state in the hopes of attending college. I was jobless, penniless, and crashing at a friend's house until I could pull it all together. I answered an ad in the local newspaper and attended what I thought was going to be a job interview. It turned out to be a sales pitch for a Multi-Level Marketing (MLM, aka Network Marketing) company.

While they made it sound amazing, I also felt super pressured. The people involved tried pushing me into getting a title loan on my car so I could buy a big starter package. I loved the draw of the freedom and money aspect, but I hated the feeling I was getting from the whole thing. I also didn't love the idea of having to sell anything, especially to my family and friends. Even if I had wanted to be successful in that business (which I seriously considered) it was impossible for me as a college student to fill my non-existent garage with products that I couldn't even afford, in the hopes of selling them... someday.

Eventually, I found a "real" job and started closing that chapter of my life just as the founder of the company was being investigated. The company was eventually shut down and the founder essentially disappeared. The whole situation left me feeling very leery of MLMs.

My story, while unique to me, was unfortunately not unique to this industry back then. It was not uncommon for people to feel pressured, betrayed, and untrusting of anyone and any company in the MLM industry. It was because of those days that we now have the term "pyramid scheme". Thankfully, things have radically changed since those early days and there are now tons of legitimate direct sales companies! However, one of the main objections you'll run into in this business (as you may already know) is overcoming people's prejudice, lack of trust, and general dislike of the industry as a whole. Acknowledging where it comes from and understanding how to overcome it will only be to your benefit.

> *TIP NUMBER 1: It is (obviously) possible to overcome the objections of reluctant people. I was the poster child for being closed-minded when it came to MLMs and here I am sharing my story. It takes time and, more than anything, it takes people being an example of the good kind of distributor.*

In the years that followed, people approached me from several networking marketing companies. My experience had been so bad, I wouldn't even listen. I had no love for their product and didn't believe their spiel about all the money I could make. One time a lady at church asked if I would listen to an opportunity she was part of and for the sake of being nice to her, I agreed. In the end, I made the presenter irritated when I told him I wanted to make a bajillion dollars in response to his "How much money would you like to make" question. I mean, who doesn't want to make a bajillion dollars, right? I'd pretty much seen it all, and at that point I could never be swayed into joining another company. I was literally the person who was 100% closed off to ever doing Network Marketing as a business. While I always wanted time and financial freedom, I had absolutely no desire to peddle wares to my family and friends.

> *TIP NUMBER 2: Don't take yourself too seriously. The gentleman who got so offended that I would suggest a number that wasn't real could have responded in a number of ways, but the one he gave was very off-putting.*

Meet your people where they are, in disbelief, in hesitation, in doubt. Your job is to help raise them up, not to look down upon them. Let yourself and your people dream big.

In 2010 I found myself desperately looking for a solution for my son's health issues. Through a friend, I bought a wholesale membership with a company exclusively for their products. I was not interested in building a business AT ALL! Aside from my skepticism of the industry, my husband and I had a full plate with our small family and running our web development business. Over the course of the next year and a half however, my friend frequently asked me if I was willing to learn about the business opportunity; to which I responded with a firm "No" every time. I loved using the product and was happy to leave it at that.

As we rolled into 2012, I felt a stirring to do something different professionally. Any small business owner knows that it is often feast or famine. At that time I was wearing too many hats, and my relationship with my husband had taken a beating. I was aching for more freedom and more than anything I wanted to do something that I felt passionate about. I wanted to make a difference; not just (barely) pay the bills.

That summer, the friend that had helped me get a wholesale membership took her approach from a different angle. Instead of asking me if I wanted to hear about the business, she asked me if I would help her. First, she asked if I could refer her to anyone that might be willing to host an event for her. Absolutely! I loved the product, she was a good friend, and I had someone that I thought would be interested. Bonus, they were! Second, she found an opportunity of working with someone online and didn't really know how to proceed. Remember how we owned a web development company? Did I help? You bet I did!

TIP NUMBER 3: In most cases, you will want to start with the product, not the business opportunity. The only reason I was willing to say yes to my friend was because I loved the product first.

TIP NUMBER 4: People are generally willing to help others out. Don't overlook your customer base that loves the product but isn't interested in the business. They are a great referral network!

I joke that my friend's second invitation actually tricked me into doing the business. The truth is that I hadn't seen a way that I could successfully do this business until that moment. I wasn't willing to do anything that would negatively impact my family, and I didn't want to invite strangers into my home. I like my anonymity and my privacy. Doing the business the way I saw people higher in the organization doing it was not appealing to me. So when she approached me about this online opportunity, I saw not only a way to do this business differently than I had anticipated, but to use a skillset I had been honing for years. I was so excited, more excited than I had been about anything in a really, really long time. I woke up excited, I went to bed excited, I was pumped all day to see what I could make of this business.

TIP NUMBER 5: Don't give up on people. Timing really does matter and sometimes it takes a year or more before people are willing to listen to or join you.

TIP NUMBER 6: Find your way of doing things. I cannot emphasize this enough! I wouldn't have been successful if I hadn't found my way of doing things. Please hear me when I say that you are unique, and you have your own life experiences and skill set which allows you to impact the world in a way that others can't. Don't underestimate that. Don't let your upline pressure you into a box. YOU - DO - YOU!

The part that was most exciting was attracting a whole new tribe of people, people who saw me as me in that moment, instead of whatever version of me that existed in the past. These weren't my family, friends, former co-workers, or acquaintances. These were people who wanted to come on a journey with me because they saw something that fit into their current life.

For many people, it's hard to make the transition from where you are to where you want to be because the people around you don't believe you can. To them you're just the sister, son, or high school friend that they saw go through all your ups and downs. If they can't change themselves, why would they believe that you could? No one in this world who became successful did it with everyone around them being stalwart cheerleaders. More times than not, it was very lonely in the beginning. The tricky part about the people closest to you is that they won't see you as someone who is able to change and develop until you show them that that is who you are. It can be a horribly vicious cycle between you feeling the need for encouragement and belief, and them not believing you can succeed until they see you do it. There is a literal breaking free that has to take place in order for you to rise up and be who you want to be. I had to do it. I know hundreds of people who have had to do it. There is a high likelihood that you will as well. Am I saying that you should avoid your friends and family? Not necessarily. What I am saying is that you should find the people and way of doing this type of business that speaks to you and allows you to be successful.

Let me illustrate to you the depth of disbelief you can run into from not only your family, but also from those within the industry and even your own company. As we started rolling along in our business and advancing through the ranks, we spoke with several people in our family about the products and the business opportunity, most of whom were not interested. Some were so unsupportive that they signed up on another team within the same company. On the business side, after hitting the first leadership rank, we were told by an upline member that the way we were building the business was not sustainable and we'd need to do it the traditional way, like everyone else. In addition to that, after walking the red carpet at the company's annual celebration gala, and being recognized for hitting the 2nd highest rank in the company, an upline couple met us at the end of the carpet and admitted to us that they hadn't thought we were actually going to succeed in the business. Amidst all the doubters and disbelievers we rose to the top. You can too!

TIP NUMBER 7: Never give up on yourself just because someone else fails to recognize your ability to do amazing things. We had been gaining a skill set and life experiences that, to others, seemed like a hot mess. In reality, it was a perfect set of events and lessons that put us in the right place, at the right time to achieve something magical. No one knows what you're capable of until you show them.

There was one major contributing factor in my being able to shut out the opinions of others and keep moving forward. It's called personal development. A lot of people know it as "self-help," which is such an outdated, and for some, self-deprecating way of classifying an industry. If you have been closed off to anything "self-help" related, let me share a differing perspective.

For a doctor to be effective and good at their job, they go through years of schooling, internships, and training to learn how to save people. At times it can be intense, uncomfortable, frustrating, monotonous, exhausting, and at the same time liberating, exciting, and motivating. This industry is no different in its outcome, but the training is a bit different. You don't have to go to school or have a degree to be successful at Network Marketing. You do have to be willing to work hard to become the best version of yourself, however. The simple truth is that personal development is the best way to grow as a person and in turn, to grow your business. One of my favorite things about it is that I get to borrow someone else's brain and life experiences without actually having to experience it myself. Being under the assumption that you have nothing more to learn is the fastest and best way to stay parked right where you are.

TIP NUMBER 8: Don't assume that you, as you are, are perfect. Being a work in progress just means that the more you grow, the more your business will grow. Personal development isn't an admission that you're broken. It's a simple step to becoming the best version of you. The common phrase "Your vibe attracts your tribe" is true. If you want a higher caliber of friends, customers or business partners, then you need to become higher caliber yourself.

The beauty in becoming the best version of yourself is that you become purely authentic, and pure authenticity is what creates a real connection with people. Sometimes it's terrifying to put yourself out there amongst your peers, but it is a necessary part of growth. We as a society are taught that we are supposed to have courage, but the key to courage is fear. You cannot have courage without first feeling fear. If being authentic, vulnerable, or showing the real you is scary, that's okay! The only version that will attract the right people to you is the authentic version of yourself. So grow. Go through the refiner's fire and be yourself! It's critical.

As you allow yourself to flow freely and do what is best for you, allow that same courtesy to those whom you are prospecting. There is nothing worse that you can do than being emotionally tied to an outcome. If you are presenting or holding an event and you're super emotionally tied to whether or not people will sign up with you, you will give everyone around you the used car salesman vibe. People don't know what your motive is, but most can pick up on the fact that you do have an agenda. It can sometimes be a tricky balance between believing that people will join you and being attached to that outcome. The best way to get people to join you is to have an honest desire to help others. When you do, it will come across that way.

TIP NUMBER 9: Check yourself. Introspection is your best (and most underutilized) friend. Figure out who you are, who your market is, and what your motives are. Your energy, your vibe, and your body language will either draw people in or repel them.

Network Marketing is, in its simplest form, a numbers game. People like to complicate it and bring in all sorts of blocks and secrets, but the truth is that once you've refined your message and yourself, it becomes simply about ratios; the more people you are in touch with, the more people you sign up. In the seven years we've been growing our Network Marketing business I have taught and prospected over ten thousand people. Of those people, I had about 700 sign up with me. From that group of 700 I've had less than 100 want to build their own business. One thing that a lot of people will get caught up in is the ones you didn't convert. If I had worried about the ten thousand people that didn't take another step, I would never have had the energy or ability to focus on the ones who did choose in. It isn't about those that don't join you. Give all your best attention to those who do!

TIP NUMBER 10: You will not be everyone's cup of tea. That's okay! You're not looking for everyone. You're looking for your people. The ones who believe in you, connect with you, and want to follow you. If you lose a prospect to another person, wish them both well and keep going.

When I finally agreed to hear my friend out about the business opportunity in the summer of 2012, I remember her asking me the same "how much money would you like to make" question that I had gotten before. This time I gave a more realistic answer. I told her $600 a month would make a world of difference for our family. Our dream at that time was to just be able to spend more quality time together. Life had thrown us some really hard and financially tough trials, and we desperately wanted to have a little financial and time freedom to make memories as a family.

The beautiful reality of this business is that when you find your sweet spot, when you're able to clear out all the limiting beliefs and all the excuses, when you're willing to push through day after day, it will reward you handsomely.

In February 2015 we went on a two-week trip to California as a reward for all of our hard work and the sacrifices we had made up to that point. That trip planted an idea in our minds and a desire in our hearts. We knew that we wanted to take full advantage of the lifestyle that we had not only created but also were endlessly teaching others about. In May of 2015, we eliminated 85% of our possessions and set off on a grand adventure with our family. Our only objective was to travel the country, connect with friends, and create memories with our kids. Mission Accomplished! It was a life-changing dream come true. It opened our minds to more possibilities, bigger dreams, and a stronger desire to experience everything else we were missing out on. This life would not be possible for us without this industry and the years of hard work and dedication we put into making it work. It is not easy, but it is not complicated. Anything worth having in life takes hard work and dedication. This is no exception!

FINAL TIP: People have asked me over the years what the secret was to achieving the success we have. The truth is that I was consistent. Even, and maybe especially, on the days that I didn't want to do anything, I still did. My challenge to you is to keep putting one foot in front of the other. One day you'll look up and realize you've created your dream life!

My favorite quote comes from the poem Invictus... "I am the master of my fate, I am the captain of my soul." Never forget, you are in control of your life and your destiny. Your thoughts are the driving force, so keep them positive!

MOMENTUM MAKERS

1. **YOU REFLECT WHAT YOU BELIEVE**: It's been said that the longest journey begins with a single step. The same can be said about self-perception. How others see us is driven by how we see ourselves. We project what we believe to be true about ourselves. If we believe others will see little value in us, we will exude a lack of self-confidence and it will translate into others seeing us but not believing in us. You have talents and strengths so believe in them and others will too.

2. **YOU HAVE WHAT IT TAKES:** The beauty of network marketing is that others have gone before you. When you join a company, you should be joining an infrastructure, with a proven product and proven system. All of the elements are there. The only thing left is your hard work. You have what it takes to be successful as long as you invest what it takes to be successful – your hard work.

3. **DON'T BE OFFENDED:** It's easy to take rejection personally. You need to understand that this business is a numbers business. Not everyone is going to say, "Yes!" But you must remember, you are not focused on your finding your "No's." You are focused on finding your "Yes's." Every single "no" is a step closer to your next "Yes!"

CLAUDIA STEPAN

FROM SURVIVING TO THRIVING

Four years ago, I was living the average American life. Married, raising three children, my husband and I both working full time hours, rushing through our days trying to juggle it all. I was teaching Kindergarten and had just finished my Master's degree in Educational Leadership, and my husband was self-employed, operating a service-based business with a few employees. Our three growing children were a blessing and our focus, and we truly weren't looking for an "opportunity" to start another business.

This is my journey to building a six-figure side income for our home using just my cell phone and social media, while working 50 hours a week as a principal and raising three children.

If you are reading this book, you most likely have an interest in learning more about the Network Marketing industry, or you are already beginning to build your dream in this amazing industry. From the outside looking in, you may be wondering if you have the time or the ability to achieve true financial benefits in this industry, and I hope that the stories featured in this book inspire you and help you feel that you can find success no matter what you bring to the table when you start.

As I mentioned, my husband and I were both focused on our careers and managing our family life. One night, after another long and hectic day, I scrolled across a social media post made by one of my mom-friends from preschool. I saw her rave about a new product she was using that was helping her feel incredible energy and sleep better at night. At the time, I was falling asleep too early from literal exhaustion, and my husband was tossing and turning all night long. So I hit the messenger button and simply asked, "What are you doing?" My friend gave me the contact information for the person who had helped her. She talked to me about the products she sold. I spent a lot of time researching the products and being skeptical to the benefits. 5 months to be exact! Finally, I realized that I had nothing of lose and was willing to give the products a month trial to see if I felt any improvements. My husband, who was athletic, and loved fitness, wanted to start the products together.

The concept of being in sales was something that I never saw myself wanting to do. The idea of adding anything more to our daily lives never crossed my mind. If anything, that sounded like even more stress! Can you relate? But there we were, absolutely loving our results and the impact it made on our personal health and wellbeing. I was so incredibly thankful for the benefits and started to share my own results on social media. Friends began to reach out to me wanting to know more about what I was using. I had so much interest, that the woman who would become my sponsor showed me that it only made sense for me to shift from being a customer to being a promoter, and so I clicked that button one month into my journey. My thought was simply, "why not?". I had no expectations or goals written down, I just knew I had something that was helping me and could possibly help others.

I had very little time in my day.   I had zero experience in sales or marketing.

Here are the qualities I did have that helped me climb to the top of my company over the next 3 years. These are the most important elements to achieving success in the Network Marketing space, no matter what type of product or service you sell.

GROWTH MINDSET

As an educator, I believe in continuous growth and learning. The moment you think you know it all, and don't need to better your talents or skills, is the moment you stop growing success. When I clicked that promoter button, I knew that I knew nothing! I only knew that I was passionate about the results I got from the products and cared about helping other people with their health and wellness. I knew that I was going to need to listen and learn from those who would become my upline who had come before me. I knew that I needed to read books that were recommended in this industry, and on personal development. I needed to be coachable.

To be successful in Network Marketing, you must take initiative with your learning! Don't sit back and wait for "assignments". I began reaching up beyond my personal sponsor and followed multiple leaders that had achieved the top rank of my company. I studied their social media content. I dialed in to their training calls. I watched their YouTube content.

Investing time in your personal and professional skillset is absolutely critical in any career. It will set you apart from those that think they "know it all" or try to take short cuts to the top. Part of your personal initiative is to take full control of how you spend your time. I had to become very strategic with it, so I looked for ways to listen to content on my headphones while doing household chores, or in my car during my commute to school and back home.

Every new level of your success is going to depend on a new level of YOU. To this day, I continue to seek ways to grow and evolve as a leader. The best part is, thanks to the Internet, learning does not require a huge financial investment. There is no official piece of paper or degree you have to earn in order to grow yourself. To win at life, you do not need a formal education. You only need to be the best version of yourself that you can be. You can learn from anywhere, at any time! If you are reading these words, clearly, you already share this paradigm. This mindset will also duplicate on your team when you lead by example! Show up to the company trainings, calls, and webinars, and your team will too!

SELF-DISCIPLINE

The second most critical quality that will determine your success or failure in Network Marketing is your self-discipline or lack thereof. Grab the closest mirror in your house and take a look at what you see. Get comfortable with taking time every day to check in with your boss.... YOU. For many people entering Network Marketing for the first time, they are starting their first experience as a business owner. They are used to working for other people, and show up to work on time, do a quality job, and strive for their best performance because someone is watching! They don't even think about showing up for work late repetitively, or simply skipping the day, because they know they would get fired! Becoming your own boss may sound like the best thing ever! No one to tell you what to do or watch over your performance. No one to call the shots or decide if you have a job or not! But the counter side of that blessing is that you have to become disciplined over yourself! With the freedom of making your own schedule, sometimes comes the ease of procrastination and complacency.

You must have a plan for your business activity and stick to it. You need to work it as if you would be fired if you didn't. Not only do you need to know when and where you are working on your business, you need to know EXACTLY what you should be doing during that time. Scrolling social media for an hour is NOT working. Engaging with specific prospects, building relationships, communicating one to one, posting valuable content, and hosting webinars are just some examples of activities that drive sales and business growth. If you find yourself frequently procrastinating, or skipping working on your business all-together, get yourself an accountability partner. Someone who will hold you accountable to do the work. That hack can help you get more consistent until you build that habit of self-discipline to the point where you don't need the partner. Remember, in business, you have to DO the DO to GET the

GET. The faster you get into a habit of daily action, the faster you will see your business thrive.

Network Marketing is unique in that you are your own boss, and you grow your business based on your efforts. However, you have (or should have) layers of leaders above you that provide support, training, and systems for you to duplicate. But your sponsor and leadership are not your boss. So never expect them to micromanage you. You want to develop self-discipline as a habit for yourself, and for the people who join you. You have to lead by example because your team will duplicate what you do, not what you say.

My favorite phrase for this quality is, "If it's meant to be, it's up to me". I start every day with a meeting in the mirror. That time that you are washing your face and brushing your teeth is the perfect time to check in with your boss. I always make sure I am able to look at my reflection and honestly be able to report that I am showing up to take action on my business each day. I also think about what's the next thing I can implement to take one step further in my business. Remember that growth mindset? It's all about doing the basics with consistency and then pushing yourself one step further.

Over the past four years, I can honestly tell myself that I have taken action on my business in some form every SINGLE day. This consistency is absolutely the factor that helped me reach my ultimate goal of the top rank in my company. It's also the differentiator I have seen amongst others in the industry. You may feel like you don't have time to work your business daily, but I challenge you to do be consistent for 90 days and watch what happens to your growth. Better yet, challenge your entire team to daily consistency for 90 days! Too many times, I see people try to go days without "working" on their business, and then try to power out hours on a weekend. Stop, start, stop, start, stop, start. Then they wonder why they can't get any momentum. I don't care HOW busy you think you are. If you can allocate 60 minutes a day, you will see more growth than if you only work your business on the weekend.

GARDEN OF ABUNDANCE

The last quality I feel is most critical is patience. I see too many people who want results fast, and when they don't get quick results, they quit before they ever really got started. The people who ultimately create long term success in Network Marketing are those who have committed to the process of "planting and nurturing" daily. I love to imagine my business as an abundant garden. As the business owner or gardener, it is my role to nurture and care for my garden. In the beginning of a business, you need to prepare the garden with rich soil. (That's the learning and personal development) Then you begin to plant seeds. These are the people you find that are interested in learning more about your products, services, or business opportunity. As you tend to the seeds with water and sunlight, (the follow up with your potentials, answering their questions) some of your seeds will sprout! That's when your potential turns into a purchasing customer. Don't worry if not all your seeds sprout! Just keep planting! Instead of focusing on who you know that isn't interested or doesn't want to be a customer or business partner, focus on finding those who do. Heck, you most likely will have people in your life who discourage you from your dreams and goals! Your closest family and friends may never join you, and that's OK! Now you continue to plant seeds daily, you continue to water the seeds and plants daily, and eventually your flower will produce more seeds and will drop them into the soil. That's when you now have customers or business builders that are helping you plant more seeds! Your goal is to continue to nurture your garden producing more and more customers, repeat customers, referrals, and business builders. This is how you create a long-term business that will continue to produce over time.

My reason for starting in Network Marketing was more of a "why not". My reason for continuing in Network Marketing is so much bigger than that! I have found a way to make a tremendous positive impact on the lives of others, physically and financially. I found a way to retire my husband, pay off our debt, earn two luxury cars, earn amazing lifestyle getaways, and most importantly, spend more time with our children. I have no doubt that the industry will continue to expand as more and more people are looking for ways to create an income without having to trade hours a day away from home.

This industry has literally taken me from surviving to thriving, and I am forever grateful for all the blessings it has created in our lives.

I wish you tremendous success on your journey!

MOMENTUM MAKERS

1. **FOSTERING GROWTH REQUIRES INVESTMENT:** Have you ever felt like something was missing? You knew you had the capability to reach your dreams but could not figure out the "how"? No matter where we are in life, we all need something we do not have to reach our next level. Before you were taught to talk and walk, you could not. So many people miss out on success only because they never put the time into learning the skill and processes that will get them to their "next." To reach a new plateau, we must learn how to climb higher than we currently are.

2. **KNOW YOUR BARRIERS TO SUCCESS:** Don't run blindly into a wall. Identify the things in front of you that can get in your way. Get clarity around your path to success and don't allow things to stop you. When you see those things coming, seek advice from trusted advisors. Others have been where you are. Don't get intimidated; find your path to "yes."

3. **STAY YOUR COURSE:** One of the biggest challenges for highly entrepreneurial people is choosing one path and sticking with it. You cannot achieve your goals if you do not stick to your path. Believe in yourself and your path enough to stay the course and not get distracted.

JO EPERE

COURAGEOUS AMBITION

As the sun is about to set on 2019, I am sitting here in complete amazement of what we have achieved, and how the life that I had dreamt up for my little family a few short years ago has manifested into the reality that we have today.

What was that life?

In a word "Freedom" — The freedom to shape each day however we choose, the freedom to spend the precious moments with our daughter Maia instead of stressing about a job that I don't love and wasting time which I will never get back commuting to and from that job.

When I stop to look back at my Network Marketing Business journey today, I thank God every day for the many blessings poured upon my family, and me but also for the awesome opportunities it will provide us in 2020 and beyond.

I was born in Wellington, New Zealand. Whilst I was not from a wealthy family, the image of my parents working tirelessly to provide for my older brothers, Sam and Eddie, and me is something I look back on with utmost pride and respect. The work ethic I saw in my parents was instilled in me through all those years; and, it has helped me consistently achieve and bring those traits into my Network Marketing business today. There is no success without a strong work ethic.

If I am being honest, I hated going to school. I would often struggle to concentrate in classes, thus becoming a disruptive student. I hated the regimented process of school-based education and I found myself fighting against that system, desperately seeking a way out. Often, my rebellion leads to hanging out with the wrong crowd and getting up to mischief.

After leaving school I didn't truly know what I wanted in life; so, due to that lack of direction and purpose, I found myself bouncing around from job to job to make ends meet. I may have not known it at the time, but those intervening years sent me spiraling down a dark hole leading to the vices of drugs and alcohol. I used them to momentarily dull the pain and they pushed me further down and prevented me from changing my life.

I moved to Sydney to remove myself from my surroundings and hopefully change my behavior; however, I fell victim to the party scene and the bright lights that Sydney had to offer. Dangerously, I became addicted to a drug known as "Ice" which eventually saw me hit rock bottom.

The key turning point in my life was when I found God via my incredible church Destiny Church. The saying that God gives his hardest battles to his strongest soldiers is one that I resonate strongly with because it is only by his grace alone that I have the opportunity to sit here today and tell you my story. I was able to rebuild my life back again one brick at a time, so to speak, and move closer towards a brighter future.

My life started to take on more meaning. I found my passion for Health and Fitness where I started in a gym as a Membership Consultant and rose to Group Fitness Instructor to a Personal Trainer. I have always been an outgoing person so the opportunity to work closely with a variety of clients was something I relished.

During this time I was first introduced to Network Marketing by a couple of good friends. The first big event I went to was in San Diego, California, a long way from New Zealand. But the trip was worth it! Seeing hundreds of different people, of diverse backgrounds walking across the stage achieving all these awards stirred something inside of me.

Whilst I was in awe of their achievements, I was very motivated personally. I started to think there was nothing stopping me from achieving all the same success and doing something I really enjoyed. Needless to say, I was pumped and began working hard to build my Network Marketing Business in tandem with my Personal Training business in New Zealand.

After three years in Network Marketing, unfortunately it didn't work out the way I had envisaged and eventually for a myriad of reasons I threw in the towel.

I felt like I had failed, which I guess is a natural reaction. This setback was tough for me, due to adversity I had already endured in my life. I had seen this opportunity as a way out and I was back at square one. Negativity and question began to fill my head and I could not find an answer or a way out of my predicament.

In 2015, my husband and I decided to move to the Gold Coast of Australia for a better lifestyle and to help our Pastors build the local church. I was still working in the fitness industry. Soon after, we had our beautiful daughter Maia.

Not long after giving birth I was back working as a Personal Trainer, relieving the financial burden my husband had been carrying whilst I was on maternity leave. The early mornings and late evenings I spent with my clients were the hours I longed to spend with my young family. Additionally, the fluctuating income of being a Personal Trainer meant I needed to look for another opportunity.

A message from my good friend Nikki was not just timely but a godsend. It changed my life. She described her new business & company to me and asked me to take a look. Whilst I was excited at the opportunity, my previous experience with Network Marketing tampered my expectations. After looking into the company, the products and having thorough discussions with leaders in our team, I started to feel like this opportunity was something different and maybe… just maybe this was what I had been searching for in my life.

The initial support that I received upon embarking on this journey and the culture of our team and company blew me away. I could sense and feel that everyone around me genuinely wanted me to succeed and they were committed to my success as much as their own. The newfound enthusiasm and passion about our business and products radiated out to everyone I connected with. I was so immersed in this journey with more opportunities to earn extra money through my hard work and have more balance in my life and putting into motion a plan to propel us forward.

I reached the third level out of four levels in our company and the income started to make a difference to our household. I started to see that this company was giving me and my family choices that we didn't have before. This opportunity offered me time freedom, I was now able to choose my working hours around my wee family.

The first event I attended with my new company was in Las Vegas and it was there where I received two prestigious awards and was recognized in front of 18,000 people for reaching the third level in our company.

It's a moment I will never forget!

But amid the personal achievements and accolades I received in my climb to the top, my greatest moment was being able to have more balance in my life and opportunities to be present with my family Beau & Maia. The opportunity I was given (and took) to smash my goals in this business means that I was afforded so much more than awards but the invaluable freedom to make our own choices in life without seeking permission from anyone else.

Becoming the first person of Samoan heritage to be promoted to the top of our company means the world to me. As I alluded earlier, it is an homage to the hardworking ways of my parents and grandparents. It is now the leading principle I am trying to show my team and the cultural people of Australia, New Zealand & Samoa.

I truly believe God has put me in this position to lead the way and succinctly articulate to them how they can become successful in this incredible business. This position I do not take lightly and is one that has me excited for 2020 and beyond to help as many people as I can.

My climb to the top of the company has been a journey of grit, resilience, patience, and perseverance and has required an attitude of doing whatever it takes to achieve my goals. It has been a rollercoaster ride which has tested my resolve to succeed and my trust in God to steer me towards my vision.

INVEST IN YOU: You must invest in yourself and commit to personal growth and development every day. I've really had to step up and grow my leadership skills and myself. Leading a team of hundreds of individuals of different cultures, ages and personalities has meant that I have had to adapt quickly. That has had its fair share of challenges; but it has provided me with real time experience to further develop, hone and enhance my leadership style.

LIVE YOUR VALUES: One of my key values is integrity; so, aligning myself with people and a company who have the same core values has proven vital to my success. If you stay true to the values and standards you set for yourself, they will become the strength of your business.

SOCIAL MEDIA BRINGS THE WORLD TO YOU: Social media has allowed me to reconnect with old school friends and work mates enabling me to continue to grow my network and build a global business where I'm not hindered by location. I have been able to build my business solely online, leveraging social media and technology, which has created time allowing my team to fit this around their work and life commitments.

Joining this company is one of the best decisions I've ever made. Network Marketing has changed our lives and allowed us to dream again and to believe we can do more and be more. It is the vehicle that has powered us to our personal goals; but, more importantly, it has allowed time freedom for us as a family, which no other job has ever done.

I'm most excited about our future, knowing this is just the beginning and having a strong vision with what our lives will look like in the next 5 to 10 years. It's an honour to help so many others. I have the best seat in the house, watching them build the life that they desire and seeing the passion and energy they have in their own journey.

Network Marketing is no longer the business of the future, it's here and It's now and I'm so proud to be a Network Marketing Professional.

My prayer is that my story provides you with hope and desire to chase your dreams with purpose and that every setback and every adversity you have faced or will face only strengthens you to commit stronger to your vision. Eventually, you will find yourself achieving more than you ever imagined if you only keep moving forward, day-by-day, "brick by brick" as I did.

MOMENTUM MAKERS

1. **YOUR CHARACTER MATTERS:** The one thing you have before you begin anything is your integrity. Keep it. When growing a business, there can be many temptations to make decisions that could compromise your character. Don't allow external factors to reshape who you are inside. You have an abundance of talent and skill. Rely on who you are, not what you want to shape your interactions with others.

2. **YOUR FUTURE WILL DEFINE YOU:** You cannot do anything about yesterday. You can do everything about tomorrow. Focus on what you want to become. Chase after the dream for your life and don't let your past trap your identity. You are in full control of who you will be tomorrow.

3. **CLIMB THE MOUNTAIN:** Just because something hasn't been done before does not mean it cannot be. Consider the challenge in front of you. It's a mountain to climb. You've climbed other mountains in life. This one is just the next one. Conquer it!

VICTORIA MCKEW
YOUR DREAM IS NEVER TOO BIG

I never would have imagined that at twenty-eight years old, I would be living a choice-filled life. My consistent dedication to the business I built as a network marketer has truly paid off. My incredible parents taught me at a very young age that the key to creating a life you truly love is having the freedom of choice and security that time and flexibility can provide. I've always worked hard to accomplish my goals and understood that a successful life requires hard work, commitment, and a never give up attitude. Before my Network Marketing business, I purchased my first investment property, travelled the world, completed a full University degree, and supported many charities close to my heart. This passion for more stayed with me, and when I began my journey into Network Marketing, through personal commitment and hard work I have created an incredibly successful business. On top of that, I have been lucky enough to help many others grow their own business, create a more balanced and fulfilling lifestyle, and follow their dreams. All of this has been possible because of my belief in Network Marketing as a business and the hard work I have invested.

To take you back, I started my business in 2015 as a twenty-three-year-old personal assistant in the Public Service in Australia. However, my real journey began two years before this when I met my partner Ratu Tagive. Ratu came into my life after he had just been unexpectedly released from a professional Rugby League contract, his childhood dream. Ratu had a challenging childhood, full of setbacks, family addiction, a gambling mother, and the responsibility of paying household bills before he even finished high school. For him, Rugby League was the lifeline he had always needed to get out of the 'norm' of his family and break free into a life he knew he deserved. So as you can imagine, being dropped from a contract at a young age was too much to bear, and after the news, he moved from Sydney to Canberra, Australia's capital, where we met.

For the first two years of our relationship life was routine for us. We both had full times jobs, I was finishing up my University degree in Public Relations and Marketing and embarking on what I thought would be the life I wanted. Climbing the corporate ladder, working 9-5, and having two days of life on the weekends. Through this period, while Ratu was working as a hotel porter, I knew something was missing. He had a 'what if' mentality. What if life had dealt me a different hand, what if I was still a professional athlete, what if I was still on the field. So in 2014, I decided to take it upon myself to get his dream back. I put together a highlights reel of his previous games, uploaded it to YouTube, and sent it to over 100 people on LinkedIn. Looking back, I was preparing myself for Network Marketing. To have the attitude of "it's not a matter of IF, it's a matter of WHEN" and to build the resilience it takes to continue through the possible rejection of your friends and family not supporting your dreams.

Three months after sending this video to anyone and everyone online, it fell into the hands of a man who played a pivotal part of our journey. He was the head coach at an amazing Rugby Union Club in Canberra and he offered Ratu the opportunity to learn to play Rugby Union in his squad, essentially as a development player. The only problem was, that at that time, they weren't able to offer us any form of payment. It would mean Ratu could no longer work full time, meaning I became the primary provider, and all the home stress fell onto my twenty-three-year-old shoulders. It was a risk because there was no guarantee that after he learned the game and played the season he would get a contract. There was a big part of me that was hesitating at first, but I just knew that this opportunity landed in our lap when it was meant to. I told Ratu to take the offer, and I would get two additional jobs to replace what we had lost from his income; so, the adventure began.

Within a fortnight I was working three jobs, eighty-five plus hours a week, seven days a week. I would go from my full-time job to a night job and double shifts on the weekend. I was trading time for money and giving up my health, social life, and happiness at the same time. It was about three months in that that I knew if I didn't change something, then nothing would ever change. This was the moment I looked into not just continuing as a consumer in my company but to take a proper look at the business opportunity. The first moment of clarity was how much I loved these products and how I already shared them with people. Secondly, the evidence of success I saw from others in the company showed me that it worked, and with time it could be duplicated over, and over. Finally, I knew it would take effort to make this business successful, but I wasn't afraid of hard work. I just thought to myself, I can add this side business into my already busy schedule now, and hopefully build it up to give me more choices. Or I can keep doing what I am doing and remain in the same place; emotionally and physically exhausted, running on empty. I truly believed I had nothing to lose but everything to gain, including my health. I rang the girl I had been a client of straight away that evening and asked her to sign me up and show me the ropes. I was all in.

That was in March 2015. Saying YES to Network Marketing to this day is one of the most life-changing decisions we have made. I truly couldn't imagine my life any other way. I had a newfound sense of hope that my life could change for the better and that I would be able to support Ratu in relieving him of any stress he felt. I was excited to start running toward my goals and had a huge vision for what was possible in this business. As soon as I started my business I was committed to raising the bar, being the voice for millennials and for those too scared to start a business of their own in the fear it wouldn't work out or people would judge them. I was, and still am to this day, the hardest worker on my team and make it my mission to introduce at least five people a day to this company and industry as we continue to blaze a trail on the market.

While it can take the average person longer than me, through hard work and putting in the hours required I promoted to the first out of only four levels of management in my company by simply sharing and selling these products with my friends and family. Additionally, my personal use helped me become an expert of the products and familiarise myself with what I was selling. I only signed up a few clients in my first month but I knew getting to the first level would help build that belief within myself and my network that these businesses worked if you worked. From there, my next goal was to reduce the extra hours I was working on the weekends which would help me get some balance back into my life and spend more time with Ratu.

I intentionally focused my energy on sponsoring a team of people wanting to start their side business also. It wasn't automatic. It took work and me getting out of my comfort zone in order to reach out to people and help those willing to hear more about the business. I continued to share and sell these products using all methods of marketing. From at-home events to one-on-one product appointments, using social media, hosting business information nights, and anything I could do to get the word out about this incredible opportunity. At this time I also committed to taking personal development seriously and started understanding what it meant to grow your mind and yourself. Once again, I promoted to the second level in the company faster than the average person. This meant I had gotten us back on track to where we were before Ratu left his full-time job. It also meant I now had the freedom of choice and the time flexibility to work my online business solely around my 9-5 corporate job.

At this time, I had also transitioned my business to be predominately online, rather than doing any at-home presentations. This helped those who struggled to find the time to physically leave the house to run their business. This transition truly changed my business and enabled me to do more, in less time; produce higher results and an international team all working online. It all seemed completely unreal. I remember getting one of my monthly commission cheques and thinking "Did I really earn this much commission, just for selling these products that I love and use and coaching others to do the same? This is the dream job!"

As time went on, I continued to work hard while watching Ratu absolutely thriving in his new position playing Rugby. I was launching business partners, helping them launch their teams, sharing the products, going to corporate events around the Country, and striving to earn any incentives the company put out for us; I was loving the journey! It was at the year and a half mark that our life took an even more exciting turn. As I worked hard to support us both through this business venture, Ratu finally received his big break! Someone in our network had sent a video to a friend in Scotland who played for a big Rugby Union team there. They called Ratu and offered him a three-year professional contract in Glasgow. I couldn't believe it. This was the WHY, this was the reason I started Network Marketing; to give us choices and to help him get this dream back. Every long day working the business and every set back was worth it. This meant that at the age of twenty-five because of my business, I had the choice to walk away from the "traditional career" and move my business without interruption to the UK. Network marketing provided the strongest sense of security because we were not chained to a physical space and time to earn a living. The mobile nature of the business empowered us to chase our dreams on the other side of the world.

Together Ratu and I moved to Scotland, ready to take on this whole new chapter of our lives. I packed up my laptop and continued building my online business from across the sea without the pressure of having to start over or "find a new job". The team I built in Australia continued working hard and building their own businesses when I left which helped them step up as leaders of their own organizations. I was so grateful that

I didn't have the normal stress of moving; in terms of how I was going to find new friends or connect with people because I already knew some of the global leaders in the UK through social media.

I landed and was ready to focus my attention on building this business even bigger. We were both living our dreams and I can say hand on heart, it would never have been possible without my Network Marketing business. The personal growth I was encouraged to undertake helped me combat anything coming my way and the friends I gained across the world helped me form a whole new network to grow my business.

Once we landed in Scotland I decided to commit my time to building this business bigger and stronger than I ever had. The best thing about running your own business is the more you pour into it, the faster it can potentially grow. I worked harder to level up my leadership, inspire others, and share these products. As a result, I reached the third level of the company which put me in the top 2%, the third of only four levels. With the time flexibility that the business offers, Ratu and I were able to explore our new home, travel on days off, and spend more time doing what we loved together. I also had the flexibility to fly across the pond to the USA and continue building my global team. I had never understood what true time and flexibility was until I had the opportunity to work my business around my own schedule. I took my health back, committed to the gym, and was able to invest in personal training and a health and wellness coach for myself. The best part was that because the business I built is both team-based and online, it never closed, meaning people can reorder their favourite products regardless of what time zone I happen to be in. Although my lifestyle was more flexible and I had more choices on how to spend my days, I still remain the hardest worker on my team, sharing this opportunity and the products that I love every day.

As things were going so well in the business and we were in such huge momentum, I committed to making my business the number one priority in my life and to work harder than ever before finally achieving my goal of the top level of my company, putting me in the top 1%. Although earning the top rank of any Network Marketing Company may not be the typical result for most people, I knew I could achieve this level of success through my hard work and was determined to be the evidence for others. This was the goal from day one, to be the youngest person in the UK to reach the top level of the Company, showing millennials that your age is just a number and building a successful Network Marketing business was down to your hard work ethic, duplicating a system and your passion for helping others. By the end of 2018, my business was absolutely booming, I was able to soak up everything I had worked so hard for and focus my energy on helping others create the same level of success I had. Ratu's career was flourishing in Scotland as well, giving us the life we had always dreamed of; him pursuing his passion for sport, and me loving what I do every day in this industry.

The year 2019 was the most life-changing year of them all. My business had gone from strength to strength over the last years and I was privileged to speak to over 25,000 like-minded entrepreneurs across different company events in three countries. I have been able to inspire and help show others what is possible in this industry which is what I am truly passionate about. Every day I am so thankful because we are helping thousands of people get started in the business each year with either our products or the business opportunity. I have complete time freedom with the ability to travel when I choose or when Ratu has a weekend off, a life very different than the one we had before. I have the ability to go back to Australia when I want to which is so important when you are living away from the ones you love. I have built a business providing more flexibility and choices than I thought I'd ever have. The most exciting part is that with intentional work and helping more people, this business has the potential to grow every month, giving me the ability to save more, set myself up for the future, and contribute in an impactful way to charity.

We have ordinary people doing extraordinary things every day in our team and company, giving hope to those who want more from life but just don't know how they can have it. I have seen people overcome limiting beliefs that have held them back for years. As a result of the dedicated work they put into their business, mums and dads have the choice to spend more time with their kids, some have gone back to study what that are passionate about, to enjoy more travel, save for a rainy day, improve their health and wellness and so much more.

I have learned so much in the time I have spent in this industry and wanted to share some honest lessons I have taken away that might help set you up for success in your business. Firstly, it is called NetWORK marketing for a reason. Starting any business is not easy, but it is worth it. Like anything in life, there may be short-term sacrifices that need to be made in order to build a business that helps you achieve your goals. Secondly, the Compound Effect is real and consistency is key when building a Network Marketing business. When I think of my business having the sales volume per month that it does that didn't happen overnight. It is the direct result of daily activity and the required effort poured into growing this business.

Thirdly, you have to recognise as you grow as a leader that people will quit along the way and not everyone who starts with you will stay for the long run. This is something that can be really hard to comprehend as you begin to build a team, but what I have learned is that everyone comes in and out of your business for a reason. And finally, the most important lesson of them all is that this industry is about helping other people. In my team, I call it 'servant leadership'. Network Marketing, in my opinion, is about putting others first with a selfless heart and making an impact on not just your life but the lives of as many other people as possible. When you can recognise that the only way to make it big in this industry is to work towards helping others succeed, then you will see the fruits of all your hard work come to fruition.

Network marketing to this day is the only industry or business I have come across that ticks all the boxes. You don't need any qualifications, you don't need to invest a lot of money, you don't have overheads or the stress of staff. You don't need to rent a space; you don't need anything other than:

- a desire for more,
- a hard work ethic,
- the ability to learn on the go and,
- the desire to share the opportunity.

In the twenty-first century, online business is taking over, people trust recommendations of their friends more than any paid advertising and that is exactly what Network Marketing is. It is an extremely simple business model, with proven results from those who have gone before you. The earning potential and time freedom that is possible in this industry through hard work and staying the course, is something everyone wants and that is what Network Marketing can give you.

At twenty-eight-years-old and newly engaged, Ratu and I have the world in our hands. We have choices beyond our wildest dreams, more flexibility than we thought possible and we now know how to help others chase their dreams too. I could not imagine life without network marketing and I truly believe everyone needs to be part of it. The most exciting part is, I am only five years in!

MOMENTUM MAKERS

1. **THE WORLD IS YOUR OYSTER:** Don't let the chaos of life control you. You get to choose what you do every day. Be intentional about how you spend your life. If you feel like the world is the puppet master and you are just running where it tells you to go. Stop everything. Take a breath. Regroup and take control of your life.

2. **REACH FOR THE HIGHEST STAR:** If you're going to spend your life working on something, work on the things that continually seem to be out of reach. As long as you are pressing harder and reaching higher, your next will always become the footstool that helps you get to new heights. Never be satisfied – always stretch yourself.

3. **DON'T BE AFRAID:** Things people don't understand can paralyze them. They hesitate or don't move at all. Don't be afraid to dive in. Whether it's social media or casual conversation. Take the risk of jumping in. The easiest question in the world to ask is, "Hi, what's your name." You'll be amazed how far that will take you.

ALICIA PESINA

GETTING REAL

The day I decided to give Network Marketing a shot…

Scrolling through Facebook, an old friend popped up in my newsfeed. She had just been promoted in her "work from home" gig she was always spatting about and now she was earning about 2 grand a month. I was like… What the heck… "If that bitch can do it-so can I!"

And so the story goes…

Some would call me a rags to riches tale; but, I prefer to think of myself as a badass with a work ethic who gets things done!

Growing up in a one stop light town with an alcoholic father and a teenage mom… the bar was not set very high for me. I had big dreams and aspirations even at a young age. I remember thinking to myself, "No way am I staying here. I am out of here the day I turn 18." And guess what — I must have manifested it or something because the day after I turned 18, I was on a plane with nothing but a suitcase and headed to the desert! My mom's high school bestie took me in for a few months but it wasn't long before I was out on my own.

I went through a variety of jobs and schools throughout my 20's. I never really finished anything and I certainly was not focused at that point in my life. My 20s were an interesting decade but a tad bit blurry. At about 30 is when I started to hold myself accountable for my choices and decisions.

I was 31 when I met my husband, Daniel. I was bartending, making good money, living alone and ready to "grow up". We had a whirlwind romance and moved in together 3 months after our first kiss. I won't bore you with our love story, but he is the yin to my yang and I adore doing life with him. When they say opposites attract - we are the poster couple.

Daniel and I were once recruited to a Network Marketing company by a local couple in financial services. We were intrigued; but, chatting personal finances with our friends was not our idea of a good time. We politely declined but the seed had been planted. Network Marketing could work...if you truly love your product or service and you're willing to work hard.

Four months after our son was born, Network Marketing found its way back to my path, back to that hot mess of a friend to join her team. Trust me when I say, if you knew her, you too would have no doubt about what YOU can do. She was a train-wreck in our younger days and it seemed not much had changed. Like I said, if she could do it so could I and so I reached out. I was a new mom and really wanted something that would let me work from home. Daniel had a great job at the time and I just needed a few extra hundred bucks.

We were headed back to that one stop light town (full disclosure-there are now 3) where the cost of living was low and we could afford for me to stay home. I began my journey as an entrepreneur. Money was ok. It took me a few months but after about 6 months I was making a couple extra hundred a month over and above the cost of my products.

The one issue I did not foresee... it did not take me long to get bored at home. So, I went out looking for a job. I am definitely not a stay at home mom. I had a few odd jobs for a hot minute before ending up at my uncle's car dealership answering phones and making coffee. The hours were awesome and I had no real responsibility. It was perfect. I was also able to stay connected on Facebook while I worked; so, I could continue building my "side gig". About a year later is when we discovered how much that extra check was needed. My husband's cushy six figure salary contract was up and not being renewed. The kicker… the monthly unemployment checks were going to total less than what we make in a day now. My side gig saved our butts. Literally. It would have either been bankruptcy or asking one of our parents for help. I probably would have chosen bankruptcy. I was no stranger to asking my parental units for help… but, I was 20 something when I did. Not 40.

It was not long after when somehow a little book, "Go-Pro" was introduced to me. This book changed my life. You may have heard of it… and if you have not, get it now. The 7 steps to becoming a Network Marketing professional. Holy shiz. I finished that book, looked in the mirror and said to myself, "You are gonna make this profession your bitch. You, Alicia are going pro." I must have listened to that book 5 times over. I was obsessed. I could learn the skills. That was figure-outable. But there was more. I knew it. The author, Eric Worrehad talked about mindset and personal development. I loved that. I was on a mission. Personal development became life to me. I was googling everything multilevel marketing (MLM) and stalking all the Network Marketing pros... then one day along came "Beach Money" by Jordan Adler. Now I get to plug my friend Jordan here. This is the 2nd book that is on my must-read list when starting our industry. This one gets your mind right. With the right mindset you can do anything. Listen to these 2 books and your life will do a 180. You can't help but change! I promise. Write your story like Jordan tells you to do in Beach Money. Manifest the crap out of some stuff. Then sit back and watch it happen! It worked for me! I wanted to meet Jordan so badly after reading that book. One day there he was at an event I was attending. I introduced myself and to make a long story short- we are now friends. I see him every week and I can call him anytime I have a question. Network Marketing can be a catalyst for changing everything about who you are and who you know. Look… Life can truly become whatever you desire. This industry can be your vehicle to get you there. You just gotta drive. Do the things, stay on course and NEVER GIVE UP.

Over the next year, I had ups and downs in my business. I hit my rank, lost my rank, hit my rank, lost my rank. It's typical in our industry even if you don't always hear that. You learn what to do and more importantly what not to do over time. Go as you grow.

I'll drop some knowledge bombs here…

First and foremost — be YOU. People know when you are faking it. If you are a copy/paster — just stop it. I promise you… a hey girl message will never get you a sale.

Set realistic goals for yourself. Start with enrolling a customer before you get mad and quit because you did not earn 2K your first week. People come into our industry and really believe they will get rich quick and not have to work. Blows my mind. I have often said God is not going to just hand you a six-figure income. You gotta learn the things first.

That is my next piece of advice. NEVER stop learning. Leaders are readers and you will never get far without growing yourself. Network Marketing is like getting a degree in being a better human… with no debt in the end.

Don't be afraid to cut out toxic relationships. Period. Toxic people suck and do not deserve any of your energy.

And last, surround yourself with people you want to be like when you "grow up". You emulate the 5 people you hang with so choose to hang with badasses. Now, back to my story… sometime later I had hit an unusual low in my business that lasted longer than normal. I was feeling a bit blah and not really feeling the vibe of the company anymore. So as some do, I started looking at other options. I dabbled in a couple. Even hit the top rank in one, which boosted my ego and gave me the confidence to know I could do it! That company did not pay or last much longer. It was just part of my process.

Then one day… It happened. Magic. I found the ONE… for me.

The universe opened up and said to me, "This one Alicia." So I said, "Ok… Let's do it universe."

I was ready. All the skills, the mindset, the relationships that I had been building on and offline… my love and passion for the industry… it was my time. Time to teach others what I had learned and grow a team of pros. Over the last two years, I have locked arms with some incredible men and women around the globe. We share a passion for our company, the products and most importantly the industry. It truly is the best industry in the world. No fancy degree needed. It boggles my mind that everyone does not at least give it a shot. It turned a kid like me into a millionaire in less than 5 years. You can do it too. All you need is some motivation, determination and a promise to yourself to never give up. Remember… If this bitch can do it… so can you.

MOMENTUM MAKERS

1. **SOLID AS A ROCK:** You must be real and you must build a team of real people. People will sniff out when you or your team are faking it. Hold authenticity as one of your highest team values. Your story on your way to success is as important as your story once you're there. Don't be afraid of the truth. Don't try to be someone you are not and don't let your team members either.

2. **LEADERS LEARN:** Seek out self-development. Every network marketing company encourages self-development. The people who succeed chase after the opportunity. They find things every day to learn and develop. If you are constantly refining who you are, you will be redefining who you can become.

3. **BUILD SOLID RELATIONSHIPS:** A chain is only as strong as its weakest link. You have a network of people around you. Some of them will be able to provide strength in your life. Spend energy and time building great relationships with great people. They will drive you and support you as much as you drive and support them.

HEATHER MCCLOSKEY

JUST JUMP

They say there is that moment that imprints on your soul forever and for me, this was that moment…

I stood there frozen staring through a foggy sliding glass door of our trailer. I was 17 and a senior in high school as I watched the hearse back up into the driveway and take my mom away. My mom was diagnosed with pancreatic cancer during my senior year of high school and within 40 days she was gone. My whole world would be forever different and the nucleus of who I was had disappeared like a setting sun.

I was numb to the world happening around me while mine was frozen in time. I was in high school. How was I supposed to figure out LIFE before I even experienced the typical right of passages of a teenager? It was this part of my life that taught me perseverance, grit, sisu (if you are Finnish you will understand this reference) and survival skills. I believe some of our greatest struggles will bring out our greatest strengths. Looking back on the last 24 years, while losing my mom was tragic, I have found growth through the experience that shaped my life differently than it otherwise would have been.

The path to finding my true purpose was not a straight line; there were so many turns, bumps and unexpected stops along the way. I am a wife, a mom of three beautiful children who will always be my greatest accomplishment; and, throughout the years I wore many different professional hats. I was a college dropout but eventually finished my degree. My focus was always being a mom first; but I also never lost sight of what

I wanted my life to be.

When I was 33, I was introduced to Network Marketing, I had very limited knowledge of this industry and held the typical stigmatic views most do. Pyramid scheme, home parties and bored moms who needed a hobby. My first off-the-cuff response was, "no way, no thanks, I'm not any of those and I am certainly not extroverted enough." I didn't walk into this industry with a huge network of people who followed, I didn't have a social media presence (unless 200 Facebook friends qualifies), and I had no past experience that would give me a leg up from others. There is one thing I did have though; I had a burning desire for change! I wanted something more for my life and my family. They deserved everything great and I was about to walk through the door to a very bright future. I just didn't know it yet.

We had just welcomed baby number 3 into our family and I was back to work at a Non-Profit organization doing my best to contribute to our growing family. Times were tough even with my husband Mike and I both working. I am no stranger to large doses of humility - I've been on government assistance, I've stood in the aisle at the grocery store using a food assistance card and praying to God that nobody I knew would stand behind me. I'm not ashamed of these moments in my life because they stirred up thoughts of living life without struggle. Everything is meant to be a teaching moment if you allow it to be, think of times in your own life where you can look back on a situation and realize how much it taught you and who you are today because of it. This has been my motto since the loss of my mom I had to see things in a new light; all things are happening for me not against me. This principle and core belief has served me well.

"Jump in!", my heart said, "What do you have to lose?" I had nothing to lose but I knew there could be things to gain; I just had no idea how much. As I write this story and reflect over the past 7 years in this industry, I never realized I wasn't just saying yes to a new side hustle, or means to making more money I way saying a big yes to me too. Yes to taking this opportunity of Network Marketing and growing an incredible income but also seeing the parallel opportunity to grow myself too.

I can list for you all the monetary things this industry has provided over the years; the family vacations, the nicer cars, paying off debt, and having more money that allowed me to be a full time mom without financial worries. I no longer worry from paycheck to paycheck but now have the ability to plan my life according to my dreams. I can tell you how absolutely amazing it is to feel worthy of success for the first time in my life, I can share how it has given me more opportunities in life like sharing my story with you through this book. What I've learned is money freedom also allows you more time freedom and, to me, that is the greatest blessing of all. Nobody can buy more time, it's our most precious commodity. When you can spend yours doing all the things you love with those you love that is the greatest gift of all.

Over the last 7 years, I've grown so much as a person because of this industry. I've conquered social media and learned that branding myself meant being myself. I've found that my true calling is leading, and I love the tribe of woman I've found, and I am more excited today about my future than ever before.

In reflection, some of my greatest lessons in life have come from saying yes to this industry. I joined with hope and a small dream to earn an extra $500 per month. As I head into 2020 with my current company, I see myself being inducted into the Millionaire's club after only 4 short years. A small mustard seed of faith has led me to this very moment. I am so proud of myself for never giving up and continually moving forward even when things were difficult.

I won't ever tell you that this has been easy because it hasn't been; but, I can tell you it has been so rewarding. Success doesn't have a destination and I don't believe you can place a dollar value on it either. I believe true success is the ripple affect you cause by showing others what is possible in their own life. When you become who you are truly meant to be, you become a light for others to see what they can be.

As I prepare my oldest child for college next fall, I see that my success, my never quit attitude, and my ability to push myself to greater heights has shown her that she can do the same. The greatest impact I have always wanted to make has always been on my family. I was never raised to believe I could do anything, nor did I have two parents cheering me on. I came from poverty and I was raised in a "barely get by" environment. I believe this industry has given me the opportunity to become who I was always meant to be. I am proud to say that my success has forever changed the legacy I will leave. I've come from nothing but yet I chose to become something. You get to decide your story. I encourage you with my favorite quote to grab a pen and start writing something beautiful too.

Theodore Roosevelt once said, "It's not the critic who counts, not the man who points out how the strong man stumbles, or where the doer of deeds could have done them better. The credit belongs to the man who is actually in the arena, whose face is marred by dust and sweat and blood; who strives valiantly; who errs, who comes short again and again; who spends himself in a worthy cause; who at the best knows, in the end, the triumph of high achievement, and who at the worst, if he fails, at least fails while daring greatly, so that his place shall never be with those cold and timid souls who neither know victory nor defeat."

MOMENTUM MAKERS

1. **YOU ARE THE PRODUCT:** People will always meet you before they meet your product. You are your own gateway to success. You must have confidence in you and your product because people buy you first. As such, you are your brand. Your product and/or company is not your brand. You must think and act like a marketer. Build the best brand you can. You will live with it for the rest of your life

2. **WORK IS DIRTY:** When we work hard, we sweat, we get worn out and tired; but that only happens if we've really done something right. Your days should end with that excited exhaustion. The kind of exhaustion that brings pride knowing that you've accomplished your goals and impacted your world. Don't ever stop pursuing the hard things to do. They make you stronger and build a solid foundation to achieve your dreams.

3. **YOU ARE WORTHY:** Every human begin on earth deserves the best life possible. Each one of us deserves the finest things in life. But, not all of us will get them. Most never know what can really be possible for them. Some give up. There are a rare few who figure out how to get what they deserve. You hold the keys to your freedom and independence. Don't give up. They are just ahead.

NATASHA ROBERSON

YOUR WHY MATTERS

How one small favor turned into creating a dream life

I don't know about you but I never woke up wanting to start a Network Marketing business. It honestly wasn't even on my radar. I was born and raised in a small village in Ohio where you worked hard for what you have, and most people were employees of local businesses with a few entrepreneurs mixed in. I was blessed to have grown up seeing both sides of this! My mother was an employee in management positions while my father was a self-employed entrepreneur. I was taught no matter what I choose to do for a career that I must love it with all my heart and work harder than anyone else to achieve the dreams I had. After college I tried being an employee and realized it just didn't fit what I wanted – no freedom, long hours and having to answer to someone I didn't really respect. Have you ever felt that way? I was an Athletic Trainer and Sports Nutritionist for an Outpatient clinic and loved what I did, but didn't love the clock in and clock out on their schedule for my life. You get me?

Eventually, I moved to Michigan and began to pursue my own story by deciding to begin my journey as an entrepreneur and started my first health and wellness clinic. At the time it seemed like the perfect moment to do this and just go for it. I had no clue what I was doing but I had mentors that would guide me as long as I asked for their guidance.

I was living what I thought was a dream life. I owned 3 studios, had 18 employees and no time to myself. I rationalized the "sacrifice" because we were helping so many people and I was in love with what I was doing. Even though I had no freedom I kept doing what I loved; helping others live the life they deserved by reaching their health and wellness goals! This led to the question many of you have probably been asked, "Are you interested in taking a look at this company I just partnered with?" Yep, one of my best friends sent that text one day. I looked at it and just went on with my day without responding. Then a few days later, she sent me another text with just a simple message, "Hey, are you free to chat for 5 mins?" Of course, as a friend I am going to say YES! I had no idea what she was going to ask me or what our conversation was going to be about. The call was set up later that day and yep, you guessed it! She asked me if I would do her a "favor" and join her team so she could advance in her ranks. I had no clue what she was selling or what rank she was hitting. But I was her friend and friends help each other out. So I said, "yes, I can help you out." I then signed on the dotted line. Yep it was still in the time of paper enrollment forms! This was the first Network Marketing Company I was part of, and I didn't even know what that meant. I was a brick n' mortar business owner with bills, employees, time clocks, insurance and payroll. I quickly realized there was little to no overhead expenses in my new side business and started thinking this could potentially be a new career path. My belief skyrocketed when I started hearing stories about the success others were having – if they could do it, so could I!

I made a commitment to grow this new business and went to work the same way I always did. I began to share with others what I was doing and the NOs started to flow in. I was like, "What the heck? this is hard!" I quickly realized I was missing the BIGGEST part of my past success in business: my mentors! I instantly went on a hunt to find the mentors who were where I wanted to be and began to learn as much as I could and ask a ton of questions.

Three years into this journey I hit a wall and wasn't sure what was wrong. Was it because I had become a mom? Was it because my traditional businesses were taking a lot of my time, which caused my Network

Marketing business to be put on the back burner? I didn't know exactly what it was but what I realized I needed a new door to open and to relight my passion for this new business model. I was feeling that "burnt out with life and business" feeling, something had to change.

I started to just go through the motions, day in and day out, and something on Facebook caught my attention. Yep, good old Facebook! After reading the story I thought to myself, "is this true? Is there really a product like this?" And then I sent a message to a complete stranger asking for more info. My first go at Network Marketing was a favor to a friend which led me to realize this industry was incredible and exactly what I wanted. Then comes this 2nd company 3 years later that I was NOT looking for, but that door opened and I didn't resist the feeling. I just went with my gut and made a hard decision to leave and start a new chapter. This new chapter felt different. I was the mom of a 2-year-old and 3-month-old, not looking to add anything more to my plate but I knew this was something I had to step into. I launched into this company with an open mind and was 100% coachable. I knew that if I followed successful people, I could create the same for myself.

Now, let me take you through those days of building this business from zero to now over $70 million in online sales with a 2-year-old and 3-month-old when I started. Yes I am married and man did that help so much! My husband did so much as we began our new journey. I couldn't have done it without him that is for sure.

You read that right now over $70 million in online sales in our organization all while raising a young family and living our dreams out each and every day. It all began with a passion to share my story with as many people as I could. Along the way, there were intense sacrifices that had to be made, many nights where mom wasn't at the dinner table because I was helping someone reach their goals. When my team needed me, I traveled with my boys. They have traveled more than most adults can say they have in their lifetime and now they are 5 and 7 years old. They only know this life and they love it as much as I do. They love meeting new people all over the world and traveling to new places. When people ask me how I did it I reply with a simple response:

I NEVER LET MY "WHY" BE MY EXCUSE.

My boys are the reason I wake up each day and do what is needed to create the life of our dreams and I will never let them be the reason I cannot make it happen. Excuses are not in my vocabulary! I have created non-negotiables that I live by; but, you will never hear me say I cannot do a call or an event for my team because I am a mom or wife. I do this career because of them. I gave up a lot of small sacrifices so we could live the life we have now. I am no longer a traditional business owner. I sold those 6 months into the journey with my current company. We had hit the top of the company 4 months straight and my team deserved more of my time, which led us to more success. With the companies gone and me working 100% on my business, my boys got me home with them! There were many nights of a few hours of sleep as my team continued to blow past ranks and still my passion continued to flow through my veins. I truly love this industry and what it can provide when you help enough others reach their goals. Your goals are going to be made a reality!

Fast forward to now with 5 years in this company and 8 years total in the industry, I have checked off 5 total vision boards and working on number 6! We have built our forever home, traveled the world, changed millions of lives, live a life by design, spend summers at the lake house and I am truly the mom and wife my family deserves full time! They get me whenever they need me! My team has my full attention because I am grounded in knowing they deserve the exact same dedication as their leader as I was given and so much more! I am nowhere near to being done and love this industry. You never know what a favor to your friend will do for you. It may just open up a world of possibilities and dreams you never knew was possible. You never know unless you give it your all and know that you are in business for yourself but not by yourself - ask for help. This industry is filled with amazing people and you are one of them! Spread your wings and make your dreams a reality. You have no limits here. The only limits you have are the ones you put on yourself.

Network Marketing is a door that when opened can lead you to dreams you never knew you had!

MOMENTUM MAKERS

1. **DISTRACTION SYNDROME – DON'T BE A VICTIM:** Have you ever been in a conversation with someone when… "Squirrel!" As entrepreneurs, it is easy for us to become equally emotionally attached to many ideas. It's also easy for us to become bored with the one we have. Distraction will keep you from accomplishing your goals. You need to pursue your "yes" to the exclusion of everything else. You will have other great ideas; but that does not make them great for you right now. Focus means learning to say "no" to the things that will take you off track.

2. **TURN YOUR ANCHOR INTO YOUR PROPELLER:** We all have reasons to procrastinate. Our "family safety" can be a motivator to not do something. Our "need for a break" can be a reason to sit and do nothing, etc. Learn to recognize the difference between what you want and what you need. You can create financial safety for the rest of your life if you take the risk of success. You can have endless vacations if you put off a 10-minute phone distraction right now. Whatever your reason not to do what you know you need to do to be successful, get under its hood and turn it into a motivating driver for your success.

3. **BE THE BEST FRIEND EVER:** You never know what tomorrow will bring. Opportunities come from unsuspecting places. Be everyone's friend. Pursue kindness and generosity. You never know what small favor you offer will be returned by the opportunity to change your life forever.

SCOTT CAMPBELL

DANCE LIKE A ROCK STAR

As a child, having a network marketing business was nowhere on my radar. When I was 6, I remember seeing dancers on TV dancing for pop stars. I was mesmerised and from that day all I wanted to be was a professional dancer and model. That is exactly what I did.

I started working professionally from the age of 18 in theatre, fashion, TV, and film traveling all over the world. I was lucky; I was actually doing my dream job and I loved it! I was loving life and living the lifestyle that comes with it.

Being a performer is not always as glamorous, however, as it seems. It has its ups and downs, as every career does. The main struggle with my profession was that I was self-employed. So, when I was working, life was great; but, when I was not working, life was still great but without the pay. I was always worried about work. Many of my jobs were short contracts; so, I was only as secure as the job I had at the time.

I always knew I would need extra money in my life, so considering another way to make money was essential to me when I got older but in my 20's I never really thought about it. Which is silly, because as a performer I relied on my body being able to work; so, having something extra like starting my own business really was essential for me.

When I approached my 30's, I really began looking at my life and the direction it was going. I still loved what I was doing. It was my passion. But I found at the end of each month, I never could save anything for the future. I really wanted to purchase a property in London. I was working hard and just never had any money left over at the end of the month. I knew I needed to make a change but had no idea how. All I knew was dancing and did not want to give up my career. When I travelled to work I would daydream about what my life would look like if I had more money and time and how that would impact me. I also felt I was ready for a new challenge in my life, where I could grow and stretch myself in other avenues. I just wanted something that could give me this and would fit into my life and complement it and work alongside I was already doing.

In 2008, I got a message from a dancing friend asking me to meet as she had just started a business that had just launched in the U.K. She was doing this part-time alongside her full-time job and wanted to meet me and tell me all about it and see if it would be something that I would be interested in. My decision to go changed my life.

The day we met she told me she had started a network marketing business, I had no idea what that was. It was a 30-year-old company that was started in the US and was now launching in the U.K. I became super excited! It felt the same excitement I would get when I went on stage.

I left our meeting that day with some products to try and agreed to meet again with her in a few days to let her know if I would like to start my own business.

As I travelled home after our meeting, I thought about what my friend shared with me. I knew nothing at all about Network Marketing, but the business model made total sense to me, and it just seemed like common sense. Plus, this opportunity answered everything I was looking for:

- It was effort-based;
- It was using products you loved and sharing them with your network who would love them, purchase them when they ran out, and reorder them over and over. That means repeat commission on each order.

- I could do it while still doing what I loved, which was my performing career;
- It could give me some extra money;
- I could work it from my phone as it was internet-driven;
- It has low start-up cost with minimal risks;
- Eventually, it could even give me more time.

The opportunity really ticked every box.

When I got home I tried the products I was given and loved them. It really appealed to me how transparent the company was and the sustainability of the products, I loved the ethics and values of the company and products.

I shared the opportunity with my family and the possibility of what it could do for me and what it could for all of us in the long term. They were fully supportive and said it would be great to do alongside what I was already doing.

But what happened over the next few days changed everything, I let my fear take over and I talked to friends about what I was about to start. They said it was not a good idea and challenged why I would want to do that when I had a good career already. So within a couple of days, I had gone from "YES! I'm doing this" to "No I'm not doing this at all", even if it was everything I was looking for. I listened to others who knew nothing about the opportunity and the potential it had. The reality was these people were not in a position to advise me on what I should be doing. The truth was I was more bothered about what others thought of me, so I said, "No.".

It took me over two years to join my friend and start my own network marketing business. In those two years, nothing had changed for me, I was still in the same position and I had not found anything else that could offer me everything that this opportunity could. Over those two years, I saw my friend grow her business and I saw how she had changed and grown as a person. Plus the company was growing in the U.K. and I kept hearing more about it. Every time I heard about the company, I just kept thinking, "You need to do this."

In 2010, I went to a large meeting and I still got the same feeling I had the first time I heard about this opportunity. I made the decision to start but still wanted someone to say it was the right thing to do. So I called my Mum and she told me to do it as I had nothing to lose and I should have done it two years prior. So, being the good son that I am, I did what I was told and jumped in.

The only reason I didn't start it the first time was due to being out of my comfort zone. It had nothing to do with the business or the products. It was all on me and my lack of confidence; but, I was the only person who could change my situation.

I started my business working part-time around my dancing and modeling career. I had a false belief that I didn't have time. But when I looked at my schedule, I found time. I just used time where I was not being productive doing something else. It is amazing how much of that there is. I stayed very disciplined with that time and stuck to my allocated windows. As I mentioned I had no knowledge in business, especially networking marketing, and I had no knowledge in products beyond using them every day. The great thing about this opportunity it is a learnable skill, you do not need to know anything; you only need to be willing to learn a new skill.

I found success faster than the average person in my company from hard work and effort I put in and built my business to the top level of management with our company. I'm not going to lie and say it was easy. I worked hard. But, when I say I worked hard, it was on something for myself and I was having so much fun at it. Some days were great some and other days were a challenge, but I knew it would be worth it. I made loads of mistakes along the way, but I learnt from them. That is the great thing about network marketing, you have to go out and do it. You cannot read loads of books to make it work for you. You need to go out and find your way.

One of the big things that blew me away when I first started was the support I was given by my friend and others who all wanted to help and guide me. I was not used to this in my performing career. Today this is something I love about our company and my organisation. The culture and community is a place where it does not matter what gender you are, where you have come from, or what you have done before. It is a culture where everyone supports and champions each other. We respect each other and truly want each other to be successful.

I believe everyone needs a sense of community and belonging. This is really how I grew my business to the top level, by making it about others and helping them grow and finding their true potential while having so much fun along the way. From someone not knowing anything about this industry, I have now built a large organisation with business in every country that our company operates in.

One of the things about this opportunity that I love is the global opportunity. When I started, our company was 30 years old and operated in just 4 counties. That made me so excited! The company was solid and stable but still had tremendous growth opportunity in front of it.

The world became my field to farm. As a performer, I had travelled to many of the places my company operated in and I still had friends there. Unlike my former career where I only got paid when I worked, by operating in a global marketplace and making the most of maximising my time by growing teams in those countries, I could now earn override commission from my team which is similar to a distribution in a traditional retail industry. Today one of the largest parts of my business is in Australia and, ironically, the friend who told me not to move forward, who is now one of my organisation's top performers, started it.

The internet and social media have made running a global business not only attainable but practical. Anyone is able to connect with anyone in any country at any time of the day. You can truly grow a network marketing business in so many ways, face to face or via social media, the potential is endless. All you truly are as a network marketing professional is a brand ambassador who is using a product and sharing the opportunity and product with others.

I am now 10 years in and my life has completely changed. One great thing about this industry is that you can create whatever you want if you work consistently. The extra money in my life has now given me choices in my life and I can still work part-time in my performing career; however, now, it's 100% for enjoyment and no longer the one thing driving me. I now have more time freedom where I can spend time with my family, friends, and travel whenever I want and do the things I want to do. The skills I have learnt along the way now serve me in my everyday life personally and professionally. What excites me most now is what is still to come and how I can now help others with this opportunity and achieve what they desire.

Looking back, while I never dreamed about having a network marketing business, it was the one thing I needed all along.

Network marketing has proved to be a very real business that can work for everyone regardless of gender and background. It allows you to have another plan for when life doesn't work the way you planned, it's effort based, it's time flexible, it's home-based where you can grow it from your phone. All you need is Wi-Fi and your voice and you can grow your very own business however you like.

Network marketing is something we all already do every time we recommend products, or services to family, friends in person, or via social media. The only difference is, right now you are not getting paid for it or even getting a discount.

If you're not already pursuing network marketing, what are you waiting for? Start growing your own tribe that creates a community where everyone supports each other.

There are 3 key principles I have lived by:

Keep It Simple: Network marketing is an already simple business, everyone just complicates it. You are joining a group of mentors with track records of success that want to teach you everything you need to be successful.

Keep It Easy: Don't create processes and systems you won't maintain. This is something that you are doing alongside your busy life, so make it easy.

Keep It Fun: Fun is one of the biggest things that I live by when growing my business. Having fun is so important as we all have stress in our li and growing your own business should be fun. Everyone wants to have more fun in their life so why not create it for yourself and others.

So what are you waiting for? This could be the one thing that could change your life.

MOMENTUM MAKERS

1. **THE WINDSHIELD MENTALITY:** No one can drive looking in the rearview mirror very effectively unless you're going backwards. So often, we think we made a decision but we continue to question it. A decision lacking conviction is little more than dating an idea. You cannot date ideas and expect progress and success. You must be all in or any investment you make is foolishness. You cannot do anything about yesterday, but you have 100% control over tomorrow. Do not let yesterdays ruin your tomorrows.

2. **PLOW YOUR OWN FIELD:** Your life is too valuable to spend it making someone else's house payment. Make the decision today to invest your life in what matters most – you and your family. If you're going to take time away from your family, make sure you're getting 100% of the reward of your effort. Being self-employed means being 100% the benefactor of your labor. Choose your life, your dreams and your passions and experience the success you deserve.

3. **DON'T STOP AT THE CITY LINE:** There are over 7 billion people on the planet and ALL OF THEM are available to you on the other end of a click of a button. Network marketing has proven to work in every part of the world. In fact, in many places like Australia and China, it is growing faster than it is in the United States. You are not limited by your circle of friends and family. In fact, they may never get on board with you. Reach beyond your borders and let the Internet be the wind in your sails.

ELISE LININGER

FROM UNSTUCK TO UNLEASHED

Although I did go from food stamps to financial freedom because of network marketing, it would do little good to focus on my success. That's the destination. The learning is in the journey. How did someone actually do it? What did it take? Do they have superpowers or are they just like you? We want the in-between stuff. That's what I want to share with you.

I grew up in Montana, and being in a family of three kids, we had a really fun childhood. We were always riding horses, hiking, fishing, doing what people in Montana love to do, which is to be outdoors as often as we can. I have always loved traveling and having freedom and knew that I wanted that type of lifestyle for my own kids whenever I had them.

I quickly learned that freedom was more precious than I ever realized. I was in an abusive relationship prior to meeting my husband. I felt trapped, alone, scared, and unable to trust anyone. I even had a hard time trusting myself for a while, resisting my own intuition, because I had made the choice to be with him. I know what it's like to be in the Welfare office waiting for someone to help me because I was stuck. I did not have that which I desired more than anything… to get unstuck - to have freedom.

Years later, I met and married my husband. We built a great life together— traveling, teaching, and experiencing new things. My husband and I love nutrition and holistic wellness. He pursued a medical career and even had a practice as a Physician Assistant. That all sounds great, doesn't it? It was, for a while. However, a medical career came tethered to student loans and way too much time spent away from the family. Long hours and big bills were slowly chipping away at our freedom. What's the point of making great money when you have to use most of it to pay off debt and don't have the time to enjoy whatever is left? We felt stuck… again.

During the winter of 2014, our area of Montana was having one of the deepest snowy winters on record. The cold weather is very hard for me - seasonal sadness, they call it. Our boys were very young at the time, and we homeschooled them. My husband was out of town at a medical conference. I was frustrated and irritable with our kids. I lacked energy. It felt like adding insult to injury as we were drowning in six figures of student loan debt and stress was an understatement. Have you ever experienced the feeling where your brain knows what to do, but your body hasn't gotten the memo yet? That's how I felt.

I prayed for a miracle.

So many times, people are presented with the exact thing they're praying for, and yet, they ignore it. They let skepticism knock it down. They let doubt poke holes in it. They let the fear of the unknown overshadow the excitement of what's to come.

It's like praying for a cake, and God presents you with the eggs, flour, sugar, etc… and you sit around wallowing in the fact that no one is handing you a cake yet. Sometimes what you seek is right in front of you. With a little bit of action on your part, you can have everything you've ever wanted in life!

Instead of waiting around, I made a decision. I decided that I was done being stuck. I desired freedom. I wanted to do something to help contribute financially. We simply had to get out of debt, fast, and I was going to help make it happen. Decision made. Now what?

I was scrolling Facebook one night, after asking God to please show me what in the world to do next… and came across a post that was exactly what I needed to see at the time.

Okay, God, I hear you. Thank you for the ingredients to make this cake.

I joined my company, ordered some products, and went all in. This is the part I feel like a lot of successful people gloss over with a "fast forward 3 years and here I am, a millionaire!". It doesn't happen that way. My success story is fast, yes, but only because I condensed about 10 years of all-out massive action into my very first few months. It starts with the decision to do the work and go all-in. Don't dabble. Be bold. I got uncomfortable when needed. I went full force with consistency and daily activity.

While building my business online by sending messages, making Facebook posts, reaching out on the phone, and sending texts, I hosted events in my living room as well. Why not capture every market you can, online and offline? Even though I live in a very small area of the country where there are more cows than people, I planned a gathering in my living room during my first week in business and invited 250 people. Do you know how many people came? Two. But I didn't get discouraged. I knew that they didn't know what I was talking about, so of course they would say no. Most people give up when they get 200+ no's in their first week. I expected that people will initially say no and it's up to me to have the vision, the energy, and the excitement for what I had found. I kept hosting gatherings week after week until the excitement caught on. The next week, we had 4 attend. The next week, 8. A few months later, we had to rent a space for over 500.

In between hosting those events, I was non-stop online and on the phone working my business into the nooks and crannies of raising our two boys and homeschooling. I was ignorance on fire, just sharing how excited I was about the products and about the business. Rejection did not phase me. A ton of people were willing to order based on the trust I had built in the past and my genuine excitedness about what I found.

The consistency and enthusiasm worked and the excitement was contagious. Soon, others were duplicating exactly what I was doing. We closed our first month of business at $45,000 in online orders. In our third month of business, we closed the month at over $200,000 in online orders which put me at the top rank of the company. That was all within 90 days of pushing the "become a promoter" button and making a decision to get unstuck.

Is it easy to do what I did? Heck no. But, if you make a decision and seriously focus on your mission as if it's live-or-die, you can do it. You will need to stay focused and stop getting discouraged when you are facing rejection. Don't let anything dissipate the fire and excitement because THAT is what is contagious and makes people want to be a part of what you're doing.

That snowy and depressing winter of 2014 that led me to pray for a miracle helped us create the life of freedom we desired.

My husband Rob left his medical practice shortly after we paid off the six figures in student loans and had a nice savings built up. Of course, he had a lot of negative people giving their opinions to him and telling him what a big mistake it was. We certainly can understand how seeing someone go from having a medical degree with their own practice to becoming a network marketing professional is untraditional, but, for us and our way of life… it's exactly what we wanted. Freedom.

We still homeschool and we are with our kids every day. We travel with them so that they can gain new experiences in life, and learn real world lessons along the way. We have even traveled the country living in an Airstream for a year! They are also seeing what it means to have a business and they get to witness the joys (and challenges) of building a business. They get to see what it really takes, behind the scenes. I am grateful that our boys are learning how to think like an entrepreneur and how to take ownership for their results from a very young age.

Much like financial freedom that you can invest back into your business, time freedom is the same. We invest time back into our team by traveling around the world to pour into them as often as we can. Although our business is all online these days, we do love being able to have the option to see our friends and team members face to face.

I have found that what holds many people back is FEAR. Mentors before me have said that stands for: False Evidence Appearing Real. If you want to be successful in your business, you must decide what you want and take all out massive action. Not just in bursts of action every now and again… be consistent. Your business will suffer if you are inconsistent. When you are consistently taking the right action, your business will thrive and flourish. Daily action produces BIG returns. Do way more than you'd think was normal. Call, text, message, email, and invite more people to take a look at what you're doing. Expect them to not be as excited as you— they don't know what you know yet!

If you're sick and tired of feeling hopelessly stuck, I hope that you'll make a decision right now that FEAR is no longer serving you. Who cares what others may think? If you need to change your situation, change your situation! Adopt the spirit of adventure. The spirit of adventure is the spirit that pulls you forward into the future like a pioneer. When you have that pioneering spirit, you get to pave the way for others and help them design their lives and live the life that they deserve. I love network marketing as a profession because I see it as an opportunity to positively impact someone's life and give them hope. When all is said and done, isn't that the most important impact we can make? Make a decision that you're meant for more…and then go for the freedom you desire and create the type of life you deserve.

MOMENTUM MAKERS

1. **Be Contagious:** People will follow your lead. Be the person you want your team to become. They will mimic your behaviors because they do not know what to do otherwise.

2. **Be An Overcomer:** Fear kills progress. Stay focused on what you know is true. If you work hard with a proven system and product you can succeed. Every door you breakthrough builds confidence for breaking through the next one. When you look back at what you've accomplished, recognize the strength you've gained, stand in that truth and move past your fears.

3. **Time Matters:** Your time is the most valuable asset you possess. Don't squander it. You can build a successful business in Network Marketing by focusing on "nook and cranny" time. You will be amazed at how much time you have to build your success in the small spaces of your life. Once you build your business, time freedom will be life's greatest reward.

Lightning Source UK Ltd.
Milton Keynes UK
UKHW020703120820
368106UK00009B/176